Navigating the Boom/Bust Cycle

Navigating the Boom/Bust Cycle

An Entrepreneur's Survival Guide

Murray Sabrin

Leader in applied, concise business books

Navigating the Boom/Bust Cycle: An Entrepreneur's Survival Guide

Copyright © Business Expert Press, LLC, 2022.

Cover design by Charlene Kronstedt

Interior design by Exeter Premedia Services Private Ltd., Chennai, India

First published in 2021 by
Business Expert Press, LLC
222 East 46th Street, New York, NY 10017
www.businessexpertpress.com

ISBN-13: 978-1-63742-119-2 (paperback)
ISBN-13: 978-1-63742-120-8 (e-book)

Business Expert Press Economics and Public Policy Collection

Collection ISSN: 2163-761X (print)
Collection ISSN: 2163-7628 (electronic)

First edition: 2021

10 9 8 7 6 5 4 3 2 1

To America's men and women who have invented, innovated, and created, providing the prosperity we have today.

Description

The audience for this book is corporate executives, managers, and business owners, for any size company; and for MBA students and executives in professional education programs and seminars to assist them better manage their companies during the boom-bust cycle.

The business cycle in the United States has been characterized by an ongoing series of economic booms and busts, bubbles and bursts—despite efforts by the Federal Reserve (the Fed) to stabilize the ups and downs. But how can corporate executives and their firms not just survive—but also thrive—when economic bubbles burst? And how can small business owners steer their companies during the business cycle so they too can thrive and survive?

This book is designed to give them tools and strategies to do that. And you will learn how to pinpoint the peaks and troughs of the boom-bust cycle to grow your business and to avoid the painful consequences of future economic downturns.

Readers will first learn what the strengths, weaknesses, opportunities, and threats of our market economy for business are; the role played by innovation, capital formation, and entrepreneurship; and the fundamentals of the boom-bust cyclical economy from the perspectives of different leading economic theories.

After that grounding in fundamentals, I will show specific tools and strategies executives can use to help their companies prosper in the boom-bust cycle.

Keywords

market economy; mixed economy; the boom-bust cycle; financial bubbles; business strategy; business planning; The Federal Reserve

Contents

Testimonials

"Dr. Sabrin presents a clear, easily readable set of guidelines and techniques to help businesspeople navigate through the perilous waters of a mixed market economy created by government mismanagement and intervention. A great read for entrepreneurs, middle and top management, and university students … and the politicians and bureaucrats who created this obstacle course."
—**Robert W. McGee, JD, PhD, DSc, CPA, Fayetteville State University**

"This is an excellent practical guide for businesspeople to help them understand—and adjust their behavior and decision making to—the business cycle. The pitch to the target reader seems just right—serious economics, data and analytics presented in a non-academic, business press style."—**Hunter Hastings, Economist and venture capitalist, Economics for Entrepreneurs, Hunterhastings.com**

"The complexities of today's business climate keep growing. Operating a successful business requires time, resources, knowledge, and skills. This book is a must-have tool in every business' toolkit. The insights, techniques, and knowledge Dr. Sabrin shares in this book will help businesses grow and set them on a sustainable path to success."—**Anthony Russo, President—Commerce and Industry Association of New Jersey, CEO/Publisher—COMMERCE Magazine**

"Dr. Sabrin, in his Navigating the Boom-Bust Cycle: An Entrepreneur's Survival Guide, brings new brilliance to the timeless Chinese saying, 'It is better to light one candle than curse the darkness.' He, on these pages, has lit hundreds of candles to illuminate every corner of entrepreneurship and economics. No longer will the reader need to stumble through the shadowy future. Every ray of understanding, here in, is at your fingertips. Enjoy and prosper."
—**Dwight Carey, Serial entrepreneur for over 60 years involved with over 200 start-ups. Professor of Entrepreneurship and Engineering, Temple University.**

Acknowledgments

I would like to thank Paul Mladjenovic who recommended me to Business Experts Press acquisition editor Ed Stone. Ed helped make this book possible in so many ways. I cannot thank him enough for his assistance and professionalism. Hunter Hastings, economist and venture capitalist, provided invaluable suggestions that improved the manuscript. Also, economist Tom DiLorenzo's suggestions were much appreciated, as were business professor Robert McGee's comments. Also I would like to thank Charlene Kronstedt for guiding the manuscript through the production process and the team at Exeter for their editorial assistance, which helped shape the manuscript for publication.

Introduction

I wrote this book to provide a road map for corporate managers and small-business owners to understand how the business cycle affects not only the general economy but also their companies no matter in what sector their businesses operate, and how to prepare for the inevitable downturns in the economy. As we shall see, recessions are unfortunately inevitable in our mixed economy, where the Federal Reserve has taken on the responsibility to "manage" the economy to provide high employment and low inflation by targeting short-term interest rates. We will examine the Federal Reserve's track record, and readers can reach their own conclusions about the Fed's policies.

When the economy is booming—or at least expanding at a moderate rate—and prosperity seems limitless, a recession seemingly comes out of "nowhere." Many (most?) business decision makers are caught completely off guard as economy rolls over. Why have experienced corporate managers and entrepreneurs failed to recognize the signs that a recession is unfolding? *Navigating the Boom-Bust Cycle: An Entrepreneur's Survival Guide* therefore fulfills a much-needed void, a guide for business decision makers to get "ahead of the curve" as the business cycle unfolds. In short, my book gives business decision makers a leg up on their competition.

The business cycle in the United States has been characterized by an ongoing series of economic booms and busts, bubbles and bursts—despite efforts by the Federal Reserve to stabilize the ups and downs since it was created in 1913. Since then, the U.S. economy had the "forgotten depression" of the early 1920s, followed by the Roaring Twenties, and then the more than decade-long Great Depression. After the seemingly endless post–World War II prosperity that lasted for nearly three decades, many companies were unprepared for the 1970s stagflation. The boom of the 1980s continued into the 1990s, and, as we shall see, paved the way for dot-com bubble, the housing bubble, and now what some analysts have called the "everything bubble."

When will the everything bubble burst? How can corporate executives and their firms not just survive—but also thrive—when the next and future economic bubbles burst? And what should small business owners do during the "good times" to prepare for a downturn in the economy to avoid a possible threat to their survival? This book is designed to give you tools and provide the strategies to do that by pinpointing when the "good economic times" will give way to the next downturn that could be as severe—or worse—as the housing bubble burst, or as relatively mild as the bursting of the dot-com bubble. No matter what is in store for the economy, you will be prepared to weather the economic storm.

As you begin the journey to learn how to survive and thrive during the business cycle, we first discuss the U.S. mixed economy with all its strengths and weaknesses and compare and contrast with an unfettered free market. Insofar as the business cycle will not be eliminated any time soon, it behooves all business decision makers to understand the dynamic factors that impact their sales, expenses and profits. With this knowledge of the business cycle they would be prepared to prosper and ride out the economy's fluctuations.

The thoughts of leading schools have been embraced by public policy makers at one time or another since the Great Depression, and we conclude this discussion about which set of ideas not only best explain the business cycle but also, provide the best practical advice to thrive during a boom and prepare for the bust.

After that grounding in fundamentals, I will show you specific tools and strategies that you can use to help your company prosper in the boom-bust cycle, including:

- Signals that identify the end of a boom and the bottom of a bust trend, so executives can tailor their corporate plans to the business cycle;
- What we can learn from past boom-and-bust cycles, and how to avoid "irrational exuberance";
- How to effectively manage your supply chain during and between economic cycles;
- How to strengthen your workforce and build an effective one more resilient to economic ups and downs;

- How to handle expansions, mergers, and other opportunities with the economic cycles in mind;
- Strategies for small businesses to deal with economic cycles;
- An understanding of international cyclical impacts on both multinationals and small businesses;
- Knowledge of probable future economic trends and how they will affect business;

It's going to be an exciting and profitable journey, so let's get started!

CHAPTER 1

The Market Economy

A SWOT Analysis

To better understand the basis and characteristics of the economic system in which corporate managers and small-business owners operate, this chapter will provide you, the business decision makers, with information to understand, predict, and strategize to solve problems as they arise, especially during the boom-bust cycle.

The United States has a mixed economy, as do many nations around the world in contrast to a "pure" market economy, which is also known as free enterprise, the free market, laissez-faire, or capitalism. There are, however, several variants of a mixed economy, different degrees of government intervention coupled with relatively free markets. There are mixed economies where governments own some key industries and intervene extensively in business. France is probably one of the best examples of such an economy. There are mixed economies that have relatively minimal government ownership of businesses and varying degrees of government intervention, for example, the United States, Japan, Germany, and so on. And there is what is generally recognized as an unfettered market economy, also known as *laissez-faire*, which currently does not exist anywhere in the world.

To provide a better understanding of the U.S. market economy in which your company operates, we will perform a SWOT (Strengths, Weaknesses, Opportunities, and Threats) analysis in the following section. It will clear up the misconceptions and misinformation that are prevalent throughout our society about business and the economy. In addition, a SWOT analysis will reveal how even our "hampered" market economy provides an enviable standard of living for a substantial portion of the population.

What Is SWOT?

Undergraduate business students typically learn how to analyze a company's Strengths, Weaknesses, Opportunities, and Threats (SWOT) in a management course. When business students graduate, they have a tool that they either can introduce to the firm in which they are employed or assist managers who are already familiar with a SWOT analysis to gather the information to assess a company's overall conditions.[1]

A company's Strengths can be summed up succinctly: what gives it a competitive edge in the marketplace? The Strengths of a business are brand recognition, high market share, quality workforce, competent management, intellectual property, strong balance sheet, good corporate citizenship, seamless supply chain, clear strategic plan and vision, and other characteristics that make the business a "powerhouse" in the marketplace.

When a SWOT analysis is performed, a company's Weaknesses may be obvious or subtle. Obvious weaknesses include the lack of a strategic plan, declining competitive position, insufficient cash reserves, operational bottlenecks, low employee morale and high turnover, declining workforce productivity, dubious marketplace image, and a "weak" managerial team. Other Weaknesses may be lack of intellectual property and poor inventory management. The matrix (Table 1.1) highlights many of these Weaknesses and a plan of action to deal with them.

Table 1.1 Weaknesses and solutions

Weaknesses	Possible solutions
• Lack of strategic plan • Declining competitive position • Insufficient cash reserves • Operational bottlenecks—inventory management • Low employee morale and high turnover • Declining worker productivity • Weak managerial team • Online challenges	• Organize retreat of key management and/or hire management consultant • Evaluate products or services vis-à-vis competitors • Review expenses to reduce unnecessary costs • Eliminate obsolete inventory and install appropriate controls to balance sales and inventory levels • Provide incentives so they can be long-term employees thereby reducing hiring and training costs • Evaluate work flow to eliminate wasteful tasks • Hire managerial consultant to evaluate key personnel • Hire a web designer to improve online presence

Companies could have a myriad of Opportunities—favorable external factors—to improve sales and profitability by entering new markets (especially overseas); by attracting successful management, marketing, and technical expertise; by introducing cost-saving techniques; by forming strategic alliances with new companies or competitors; by getting "ahead of the curve" as consumers' tastes and preferences change; and being attuned to the unfolding political and macro-economic trends that could impact your operations. Overall, in the 21st century, companies may have to "reinvent" themselves by downsizing, reducing, or eliminating their brick-and-mortar stores and boosting their e-commerce. In short, astute and company business analyst or consultant must in effect be a "jack of all trades" who understand the economy's Big Picture and can identify—and embrace—the Opportunities that propel businesses to greater success. Table 1.2 illustrates this approach.

If competition is a "war," then there are plenty of landmines so to speak that could pose as lethal or debilitating Threats—factors that can harm performance and undermine a business' future. An impending recession, foreign competition, financially stronger competitors, new technology, or obsolete product or service could threaten a company's future, as well as competitors poaching its management and technical experts. Moreover, is the market for the company's products or services decelerating? Are

Table 1.2 Opportunities and actions

Opportunities	Possible actions
• Expand locally, regionally, nationally, and overseas • Form strategic alliances overseas • Target new demographic market • Merge with a competitor or a firm in the supply chain • Purchase a successful or struggling competitor • Hire experienced managers	• Research domestic markets and/or hire consultant for overseas expansion • Hire consultant who can investigate overseas firms for alliances • Evaluate marketing trends to expand into new demographics • Determine what firms would provide synergies, whether a competitor or a firm in the supply chain • Be on the look out for a competitor that may be for sale or a struggling competitor that may have valuable assets • Network with firms in your industry for a possible "star" to join your company and/or use an online recruiter

the marketing experts unaware of changing tastes and demographic shifts that are impacting the company's sales and bottom-line?

Uses of SWOT

A SWOT analysis can help business decision makers pinpoint where they should focus their attention to improve their firm's performance. The internal issues highlight the strengths and weaknesses of a company. Business decision makers should obviously build on the strengths and address as quickly as possible the weaknesses to improve the company's prospects. By the same token, decision makers must be aware of the external factors—opportunities and threats—that would improve the business' sales and profitability and be mindful of the threats that could undermine their companies' permanency. The history of American business unfortunately reveals how one-time iconic companies—and products—have fallen by the wayside.

A SWOT analysis of the whole economy can provide business decision makers with the "macro" perspective about the ebbs and flows of the business cycle, which have widespread impacts on virtually all sectors. Thus, knowing where we are in the business cycle could provide valuable information for a business decision maker to plan appropriately and avoid the consequences of an economic downturn, which could turn profitability into substantial losses.

Examples of SWOT

Although SWOT provides an easily understandable general and easy-to-use method to highlight the internal and external factors affecting a business, additional information is needed to "drill down" to obtain the specific issues that should be addressed to create a better company.[2] Nevertheless, by having an initial framework for distilling a company's overall performance, analysts like Kenneth J. DeFranco, Jr. have used a SWOT to highlight, for example, Coca-Cola's business strengths and challenges.[3] DeFranco's succinct analysis highlights the key aspects of each SWOT component after providing a brief history of the company. At that time, the author concluded that "conservative investors wanting a reliable source of income and a bit of capital gains exposure might want to give the Coca-Cola Company a glance." Needless to say, a SWOT analysis is not a foolproof method for investor success but a good starting point to determine if the company's stock is indeed a "buy" based upon a comprehensive evaluation of its Strengths, Weaknesses, Opportunities, and Threats.

A SWOT, therefore, can be used by internal analysts to improve the company's prospects but also by financial analysts who provide guidance for investors. Additional SWOT analyses for 30 well-known companies—from Amazon to Facebook to Walt Disney—can be found at https://strategicmanagementinsight.com/swot-analyses.html. The website highlights a portion of the SWOT analysis and the rest can be purchased online.

The Market Economy: A SWOT Analysis

A Google search of a market economy and SWOT analysis does not provide any tangible results. However, a Google search of advantages and disadvantages of a market economy yielded more than 41 million results. It would take several lifetimes to review all the results of such a search. Nevertheless, a perusal of the common themes can be used to create a SWOT of the market economy.

A market economy's Strengths, Opportunities, and Threats are obvious given some critical thought and examination of the subject. However, critics of a "pure" market economy assert there are Weaknesses that should be corrected by government policies, which will be cited in the SWOT matrix.

A free market economy nevertheless has many advantages over a *command economy*, where the government typically controls virtually all production and distribution of goods and services. The former Soviet Union and China before its economic reforms are examples of a command economy as is Cuba and North Korea today. All noncommand economies in the world today are *mixed economies*, where government owns or controls such sectors as railroads, airlines, utilities, highways, medical care, education, and other key activities. In a mixed economy, numerous government agencies, bureaus, departments, and so on regulate the private sector. The government intervenes in the economy with regulations that impact wages, prices, working conditions, and so forth. Most policy makers and many economists in the United States, Europe, and other regions typically support a *mixed economy*, claiming a mixed economy is preferable to a "hands-off" or laissez-faire economic system.

A SWOT of a free market economy (see Tables 1.3 and 1.4) resulted in the following analysis. The Strengths, Opportunities, and Threats and the subsequent discussion highlight how a free market economy would provide boundless opportunities for both large and small businesses and sustainable prosperity. The Weaknesses cited in the matrix are those of free market critics who claim that a mixed economy would eliminate the flaws they have identified (see Table 1.3).

Strengths

A free market's Strengths can be summed up from the SWOT. In an unhampered market economy, entrepreneurs invest in productive enterprises to provide consumers with the goods and services that they value the most. Without burdensome regulations and low taxes, the theory of free markets asserts that an economy would achieve the highest living standards for both entrepreneurs and workers.[4] Thus, according to the advocates of free markets, curbing government intervention in the economy would produce sustainable prosperity.

Weaknesses

Critics of the market economy assert that income and wealth inequality, business monopolies, pollution, the boom-bust cycle, and insufficient spending on education and public health are some of the negative consequences of laissez-faire economics. Economists in this camp generally support government policies to correct the "deficiencies" of a market economy. Other critics claim that a market economy lacks a firm moral foundation and therefore government intervention is necessary to combat what is viewed as the counterproductive "selfishness" and individualism of the free market. In short, according to this perspective, a free market does not promote a compassionate collective spirit and therefore should be tempered by enlightened social and economic policies.[5]

Natural income inequality occurs because some people have more talent, skills, or entrepreneurial drive than others. Professional athletes,

Table 1.3 SWOT analysis of a free market economy

Free market economy Internal	
Strengths	**Weaknesses (according to critics of free markets)**
• Voluntary exchange • Price discovery • Private property rights assigned • Entrepreneurship • Capital investment and accumulation • Free trade • Financial markets • Competition • Higher real wages • Increasing living standards • Sustainable prosperity • Freedom to innovate • Peaceful international relations • Cooperation among market participants • Consumer sovereignty • Human capital development	• Income inequality • Monopolies • Stagnant wages • Pollution • Underfunding of public sector • Health care disparities • Prone to boom-bust cycle • Unemployment crises • Market failure in some sectors • Insufficient regulations of business • Racism
Opportunities	**Threats**
• Boundless penetration of domestic and international markets • Create quality products and services • alternatives to government services	• Central bank manipulation of interest rates and creation of new money • Taxes • Regulations such as price controls, antitrust laws, minimum wage, professional licensing (to name a few) • Trade barriers • Tariffs • Eminent domain • Lockdowns • Political resource allocation
External	

entertainers, and self-made entrepreneurs as well as competent business executives—CEOs, CFOs, and other upper-level management—earn substantial multiples of the average individual income in our country. Individuals are highly compensated because of their talents. Interestingly enough, professional athletes and entertainers are rarely criticized for their multimillion-dollar annual incomes while corporate executives on occasion are excoriated—sometimes justifiably when they are fired for mismanaging a business with a so-called golden parachute—for their high salaries and stock options. Nevertheless, in a free market, "income inequality" is not a "weakness" but a reflection of reality that individuals with enormous talents in different fields are compensated handsomely.

One of the most pervasive criticisms of a market economy is that it is prone to some businesses obtaining "monopoly power." Historically, however, monopoly has meant a grant by the state to a company for the exclusive production or sale of a product or service in a specific geographic area. In other words, monopolies are not creatures of the free market but of government intervention. A business with substantial market share is not in and of itself proof of "monopoly power." Even companies with a huge market share cannot dictate prices to consumers, because in the final analysis a business cannot raise prices more than what consumers are willing to pay. In short, in a market economy, consumers in effect "dictate" prices to businesses. Any business executive or small business owner knows that raising prices will tend to reduce demand for their product or service.

A free market economy, according to some critics, creates "externalities" such as pollution and therefore requires regulations to stop businesses from despoiling the environment. However, if pollution is considered a type of "trespass," then the legal system should deal with this problem through lawsuits to prevent a polluter from committing noxious, toxic particles in the air and discharging water and other substances into rivers, lakes, and streams. In short, in a free market, property rights would be strictly enforced and the courts would punish polluters by making them pay for the damages they inflict on nearby property owners and the general public.[6]

A common complaint leveled at a market economy is that insufficient resources are "invested" in public education and health care. As far as public education is concerned, governments do not invest but spend other people's money and therefore the money spent on public education is not a weakness of the free market but a criticism of the cost and structure of public education, namely, in some communities the cost per pupil is more than $25,000 per year.[7]

The cost of American health care as a percentage of GDP is the highest in the world. Our "hybrid" system of private employer-based insurance and government programs such as Medicare, Medicaid, and Obamacare subsidies now accounts for 18 percent of GDP, up from less than 7 percent 55 years ago, when both Medicare and Medicaid were enacted in the Johnson administration.

Opportunities

A market economy flourishes when entrepreneurs have the freedom to invest, innovate, produce, and trade—domestically and internationally—in order to meet consumers' needs. Thus, fewer regulations, lower taxes, eliminating trade barriers, and financial stability create an environment for sustainable prosperity.

President Carter's administration in the late 1970s undertook an extensive deregulation of major sectors of the U.S. economy, which unleashed the creativity of American entrepreneurs, and the slaying of the inflation dragon by then Federal Reserve Chairman Paul Volcker created conditions for a booming 1980s. For more than four decades since the Carter deregulation policies, consumers have benefited from the increase in competitive forces, which have led to lower prices in telecommunications, transportation, and other sectors that were stifled by the federal government's interventionist policies.[8]

In the health care sector, even before the pandemic of 2020 revealed the weaknesses in the American health care system, physicians and entrepreneurs have begun to implement free market medical care all across America.

Physicians who were unhappy with the traditional medical practice where they would have approximately 2,000 patients and spend very little time with each patient opted out and created a Direct Primary Care (DPC) practice (https://www.aafp.org/home.html). In a DPC practice, a physician would typically have no more than 700 to 800 patients. Patients pay a relatively modest monthly fee and have access to the physician virtually 24/7. Neither patients nor physicians would have to file an insurance claim in a DPC practice, thus reducing the number of administrative staffers needed in office. At Forward, also a fee-only practice with offices in several major cities, innovative state-of-the-art diagnostic tests discover medical issues that could be treated before the onset of an irreversible chronic condition (see the Forward website, https://goforward.com).

Other free market innovations in health care include the Surgery Center of Oklahoma, which provides high-quality services at a fraction of the prices insurance companies pay in a typical hospital setting (https://surgerycenterok.com).

At Medibid.com, physicians literally bid for patients' "business" bypassing insurance companies—the middleman—and charge much lower prices than a typical hospital-based procedure. And at Christian Ministries, individuals and families "pool" their funds to pay for the medical bills of their members. Although faith-based Ministries are not technically medical insurance, they are a throwback to the mutual aid societies of the 19th and early 20th centuries of community solutions to social and economic challenges (see https://www.chministries.org).

Although the pandemic of 2020—or more accurately the lockdowns throughout the country to halt the spread of the virus—caused businesses throughout the economy to close, from restaurants to mom-and-pop shops on Main Street to major retailers such as JCPenney and Lord & Taylor, new businesses emerged or expanded to meet consumer demands in the age of COVID.[9] Companies such as Zoom, Etsy, Carvana, Restoration Hardware (now named RH), and dozens more engaged in e-commerce or filling a niche or void because of the disruptions have seen their common stock rise substantially throughout 2020.

Threats

Several years ago, Warren Buffett noted, "we will have periodic recessions and occasional panic but the good news is in the 20th century, we had two world wars, the flu epidemic, the Cold War, atom bomb, you name it. And the Dow Jones [Industrial Average] went from 66 to 11,004. All these terrible things happened, but America works."[10] We had the dot-com bubble, the housing bubble, and the deepest financial crisis since the Great Depression; the pandemic of 2020, which saw the U.S. economy contract by more than a 30 percent annual rate in the second quarter of the year and the unemployment rate jump to the highest level since the 1930s. Clearly, in the face of a public health crisis and periodic financial bubbles, the resiliency of the U.S. economy cannot be denied.

According to an annual survey published by the Competitive Enterprise Institute, *Ten Thousand Commandments*, an ongoing threat facing the U.S. economy is the more than $1.9 trillion cost of federal regulations (Crews, 2020). To put the costs of federal regulations in perspective, the annual survey points out that federal regulations cost each U.S. household $14,000 annually, which "equals about one-fifth (18 percent) the average pretax household budget as the second biggest budget item after housing." The estimated $1.9 trillion regulatory cost is slightly less than the "$2.5 trillion COVID-19 Phase 3 stimulus bill Congress passed in April 2020." A bright spot in the annual survey is that the number of pages in the Federal Register declined during the Trump administration to an average of 66,490 pages per year, substantially less than the annual average of 80,420 pages during President Obama's presidency.[11]

Additional threats that could undermine rising living standards include trade wars, increased federal spending accompanied by huge budget deficits, and monetization of the federal debt by the Federal Reserve, all of which have the potential to cause higher price inflation and rising interest rates. The debt/GDP ratio has been on an upward trajectory since the dot-com bubble burst in 2000. Historically, rising debt levels and central bank monetization of the debt have created widespread dislocations in both production and the labor force.

The Mixed Economy: A SWOT Analysis

Although the United States has never been an unfettered, laissez-faire economy, our mixed economy has "delivered" the goods for several decades despite being hampered by interventionist public policies. Real GDP has increased markedly since the end of World War II even as periodic recessions put a temporary halt in the rise of goods and services. Suffice it to say, Warren Buffett's observation at Berkshire's 2019 annual shareholder meeting—billed as the Woodstock for Capitalism—was spot on, "I believe we wouldn't be sitting here except for the market system."[12]

A country that has an unhampered, unfettered, laissez-faire economic system is a "pure" market economy. All the Strengths of a market economy would be in full bloom if government intervention were kept at a minimum or nonexistent. Mises' insightful book was written in 1940 and then translated from the original German decades later. His analysis highlights the so-called third way between capitalism and socialism, which he dubbed "interventionism," and why it is not a viable alternative to a pure market economy. In contemporary economic discourse, interventionism is usually described as a mixed economy.[13] I have described the internal and external characteristics of a mixed economy in Tables 1.3 and 1.4, respectively.

Sound economic analysis requires a thorough understanding of the effects of government intervention. Instead of asserting that a mixed economy is "superior" to a market economy by "smuggling" ethical judgments

Table 1.4 Mixed economy: Internal and external characteristics

Mixed economy	
Strengths	**Weaknesses** **(according to critics of mixed economy)**
• Voluntary exchange • Price discovery • Private property rights generally assigned • Entrepreneurship • Capital investment and accumulation • Free trade • Financial markets • Competition • Higher real wages • Increasing living standards • Freedom to innovate	• Income inequality caused by monetary inflation and regulations • Monopolies (state sanctioned) • Stagnant real wages • Bloated public sector • Health care distortions • Prone to boom-bust cycle • Overbearing business regulations • Domestic and international trade restrictions
External	
Opportunities	**Threats**
• Boundless penetration of domestic and international markets • Create quality products and services alternatives to government services	• Central bank manipulation of interest rates and creation of new money • Persistent business cycles • Taxes • Regulations such as wage-price controls, antitrust laws, minimum wage, professional licensing (to name a few) • Trade barriers • Tariffs • Lockdowns • Eminent domain • Political resource allocation

into their analyses, critics of free markets have left themselves open to a valid rejoinder. Namely, how would a mixed economy, which requires a vast bureaucracy to implement, create optimal outcomes in production, employment, and consumption?

Proponents of a mixed economy do not address the weaknesses inherent in an interventionist economic system but instead rely on unwanted assertions and dubious ethical objections to criticize a pure market economy.[14]

Economist Robert Higgs applied insights about interventionism in his analysis of how government grows. As Higgs points out, "There was a time, long ago, when the average American can go about his daily business hardly aware of the government—especially the federal government. As a farmer, merchant, manufacturer, he could decide what, how, when, and where to produce and sell his products, constrained by little more than market forces."[15]

Higgs reviews the theoretical underpinnings of the growth of government and then pivots to the historical changes that transformed America from a relatively laissez-faire economy in the 19th century to a mixed economy that has grown with every periodic crisis since then. Those crises include war and the Great Depression, and the ideological shift of policy makers to a more interventionist mindset that laid the foundation for President Johnson's Great Society programs.

Innovation, Capital Formation, and Entrepreneurship

A mixed economy like the United States, even with the counterproductive interventions governments have imposed throughout our history, has had an incredible number of innovators and creative and forward-looking entrepreneurs, generation after generation. A robust financial system has provided the necessary capital to take ideas from the laboratory and the proverbial basement or garage to the marketplace. Next, we shall see how the essential factors of our economy have been able to create goods and services for the masses.

Innovation

Innovation, simply put, is doing things better; Henry Ford's assembly line is probably the most well-known idea that was implemented and literally revolutionized the manufacturing process. As historian and journalist Harold Evans points out, "Innovation … has turned out to be a distinguishing characteristic of the United States. It is not simply innovation; it is inventiveness put to use."[16] Evans' sweeping survey of America's inventors, innovators, and entrepreneurs begins with John Fitch and the first steamboat in America and ends with Larry Page and Sergey Brin, cofounders of Google. In between, Evans highlights the enormous contributions of scores of men and women who transformed America from a vast untamed continent to the economic powerhouse it is today—in just over two centuries. Although other countries have also been endowed with natural resources—Russia, China, Australia, Canada, Brazil, Argentina, and South America—Evans attributes America's success to what he calls the "genius for innovation."

For example, Robert Watson Watt invented radar in England in 1935, which was instrumental in helping the British win the Battle of Britain in World War II. Nevertheless, it was American innovators who ran, so to speak, with the radar technology and created the electronics industry. Other British inventions and discoveries—penicillin (1928), jet propulsion (1930), and commercialization of computers (1951)—became the basis of American innovation and industrialization. Clearly, innovation is insufficient for ideas to be transformed into great companies and industries.

Another key feature of innovation is the "democratization" of goods and services. Evans points out how banking, photography, e-mail and the Internet, computers, and a host of other goods and services that originally were only available to the economic elites in the country became accessible to the so-called common man. Innovators not only were interested in profits but by a sincere desire to improve the lives of the masses by keeping prices affordable.

Forbes magazine has compiled lists of the most innovative companies, ideas, and American leaders.

In 2020, the five most innovative companies, according to the Boston Consulting Group (BCG), were household names—Apple, Alphabet, Amazon, Microsoft, and Samsung—as you would expect.[17] Not surprisingly, the top five companies are all in the broad category of technology, either creating hard goods or applications or providing services for both consumers and businesses. Samsung, the only non-American company, was founded in 1938, while the four American companies were founded within the past 45 years. Other well-known international companies on the list of the 50 most innovative companies of 2020 include Alibaba, Sony, SAP, Hitachi, Tencent, and Volkswagen. Some of the U.S. companies that made the list include IBM, Facebook, Tesla, Walmart, Costco, and Dell.

According to the BCG report, the top innovative companies focus their strategies to take advantage of opportunities when economic downturns occur and thus have been able to provide superior returns to investors over the long term.[18]

Innovative companies would not be successful without farsighted leaders who take a long-term view of implementing their vision. Heading up the list are Jeff Bezos, Elon Musk, Mark Zuckerberg, Marc Benioff (Salesforce), and Reed Hastings (Netflix). The compiled list of America's 100 top innovative leaders is based on several metrics but the one that stands out is creating both value for consumers and high returns for both investors.[19] In short, the innovators of the current era are no different than the 18th-, 19th- and 20th-century innovators—they took an idea and transformed it into a valuable good or service by making it available to the masses.

Lastly, *Forbes* compiled a list in order of importance of the most innovative products and services of the past three decades based on the Public Broadcasting System show the *Nightly Business Report* on the celebration of its 30th anniversary on the air.[20] Virtually everyone on the planet has been touched by a multitude of innovations both at home and in the workplace. Worker productivity has increased immeasurably as data and information have become easily accessible and stored efficiently. People have been able to communicate seamlessly through the Internet at a fraction of the costs in previous eras. In fact, in addition, countless lives have been saved and prolonged because of early diagnosis of diseases, which made effective treatment possible. Moreover, the pandemic of 2020 has increased the use of remote learning and conferencing as well as telemedicine. The events of the past three decades are a testimony to the endless innovations that have been a hallmark of the American experience.

Entrepreneurship

Inventors and innovators as brilliant as they are must also have the drive and perseverance to turn their ideas to products and services in the marketplace. The innovators on the *Forbes* list are also entrepreneurs, the "movers and shakers," who act upon their vision to build a sustainable business until the next disruptor comes along. They had an idea, from Jeff Bezos who began selling books through the mail, which has since blossomed into an e-commerce behemoth, to Mark Zuckerberg who created a social media platform connecting billions of people from around the world who otherwise would probably never have met, to Reed Hastings CEO of Netflix, which began as DVD mail rental business and now oversees one of the most successful live streaming services in the world that also creates its own content.

One of the most well-known examples of an entrepreneur who took an already existing idea, the McDonald brothers' San Bernardino, California, restaurant menu of only hamburgers, fries, and drinks and turned it into one of the most visible brands in the world, McDonald's. Ray Kroc began franchising McDonald's restaurants in the mid and late 1950s after he witnessed the quality and service of the brothers' operation, and in 1961 bought the exclusive rights to the McDonald's name and operating system. And as they say, the rest is history.

The McDonald brothers were both innovators and entrepreneurs. Their restaurant operating system became the model for other restaurant chains to emulate. But instead of joining Ray Kroc in taking McDonald's to the next level, which eventually became one of the most iconic consumer brands in the world, the brothers were content to sell their rights to Kroc who became one of the great entrepreneurs in American history. Kroc in effect democratized fast food in the United States and brought his entrepreneurial vision to the rest of the world.[21]

Capital Formation

Capital can be described as simply as the "stuff" that makes other "stuff." In other words, everything from machinery, factories, transportation equipment, and other "capital goods" which are essential to create products for eventual sale to consumers at the retail level constitute the capital goods sector. The factors of production include the following: Land—physical and natural resources; Labor—blue- and white-collar workers; Capital—factories, machinery, transportation equipment, materials, and intellectual property.

Another critical component not only for capital formation but also for an economy in general, without which industrialization would be impossible is money. At each step of the production process, money is exchanged to purchase raw materials, invest in capital goods, hire workers, pay for research and development, and pay dividends to shareholders. In addition, businesses need money to pay their taxes. A market economy is in effect a countless number of monetary transactions throughout the structure of production, from extracting resources to retail sales. In our $20 trillion economy, with a population of 330 million people, a reliable payments system is the "grease" that makes the economy run as smoothly as it does.

Capital formation occurs when individuals—and businesses—first save and then invest. The act of saving is an essential step in the capital formation process. Savings are then invested directly into businesses, which is better known as venture capital, as entrepreneurs use the funds to build or expand their enterprises. The founders of Apple, Google, Facebook, and other contemporary companies and the entrepreneurs—Ford, Carnegie, Rockefeller, and others—of bygone eras tapped the savings of friends and family and others who provided the financial resources they needed to get their businesses off the ground. Once a company is established, it can then tap the capital markets for additional resources, where the general public can invest their capital in an initial public offering (IPO) and/or purchase a company's bond, which could be used for additional capital goods purchases. The banking system also channels the public's savings into loans for entrepreneurs. In addition, a portion or all of a company's profits can be plowed back into the business (retained earnings), another form of savings.

Capital formation therefore provides several major benefits for a market economy. It increases worker productivity and thus their real wages; it lowers the cost of production and thus helps drive down prices making more goods affordable for the masses; it makes possible for innovators to see their ideas become realities in the marketplace. In short, capital formation is indispensable for both innovators and entrepreneurs to satisfy the needs of the people and thus increase their living standards. Without capital formation, living standards would be near the subsistence level throughout the world. A free market, with a vibrant capital market, provides the framework for a growing economy. Any interference with the capital formation process lowers living standards from what they would otherwise be. Critics of the free market, who tend to ignore the consequences of their interventionist policy prescriptions, disregard the crucial role capital formation plays in the economy.

The private nonresidential fixed investment in the United States since the end of World War II has grown from $25,000,000,000 to more than $2.6 trillion today. In fact, it correlates step-by-step with the growth of real GDP (see Figure 1.1), revealing how an economy must invest in capital before goods and services can be consumed by the masses. There is no shortcut to creating consumer goods without an enormous investment in capital good, which is one of the most important lessons of economics and business.

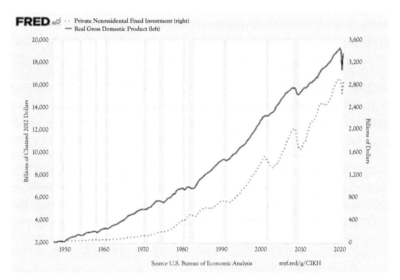

Figure 1.1 The growth of real GDP and investment

Source: U.S. Bureau of Economic Analysis, Real gross domestic product [GDPC1], retrieved from FRED, Federal Reserve Bank of St. Louis; https://fred.stlouisfed.org/series/GDPC1, March 24, 2021.
U.S. Bureau of Economic Analysis, Private nonresidential fixed investment [PNFI], retrieved from FRED, Federal Reserve Bank of St. Louis; https://fred.stlouisfed.org/series/PNFI, March 24, 2021.

CHAPTER 2

The ABCs of the Boom-Bust Cycle

There are four main theories of the business cycle: Keynesian, Monetarist, Supply Side, and Austrian. Let me explain each one, highlight the differences, and suggest which is the best lens for businesses to look through.

The boom-bust cycle—also called "panics" for many decades—has been a recurring phenomenon since the early days of the Republic. There were 13 financial panics from 1792 to 1896,[1] and the last official one occurred in 1907.[2] Since then, the boom-bust cycle has occurred periodically and the previous panics were renamed, first to *depression* and then to the milder sounding term, *recession*.

Soon after the recovery from the Panic of 1907, the U.S. economy boomed during World War I as companies were supplying food and goods to European nations. After the Great War ended in 1918, a year after the United States entered the war, the federal government had borrowed heavily from the American people and the newly established Federal Reserve (the Fed) printed money as well to assist financing the war effort, a major economic downturn, the so-called Forgotten Depression (1920–1921) occurred. The depression was over without any "stimulus" spending by the Harding administration.

After the seemingly unstoppable prosperity of the 1920s, the economic downturn that began in 1929 came "out of the blue" and lasted more than a decade. After the end of World War II, any future economic slump would now be called a "recession" to avoid memories of the prolonged slump of the 1930s.

An occasional mild downturn interrupted America's postwar prosperity until the severe recessions of the 1970s. At the dawn of the 21st century, the dot-com bubble (a bubble unfolds when one or more assets increase at unsustainable rates) occurred. That was followed by a relatively

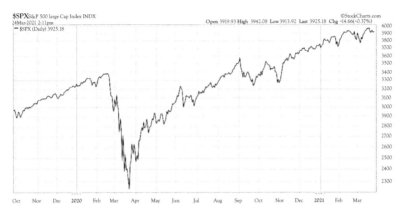

$SPX S&P 500 large Cap Index INDX   ©StockCharts.com
24-Mar-2021 2:11pm   Open 3919.93 High 3942.08 Low 3913.92 Last 3925.18 Chg -14.66(-0.37%)
— $SPX (Daily) 3925.18

Figure 2.1 Stock prices snapped back from early 2020 pandemic low

Chart courtesy of StockCharts.com

mild, short recession (March–November 2001), which in turn was followed by the housing bubble and the Great Recession (December 2007–
June 2009). The next phase of the business cycle has been dubbed the
"everything bubble."[3] The stock market, the bond market, and other asset
prices roared ahead until early 2020 when the pandemic hit America and
the rest of the world, causing a severe drop in U.S. stock prices (February
12–March 23). The snapback from the pandemic low has been equally
impressive so far (see Figure 2.1).

Why is it important to understand the boom-bust cycle? The business
cycle is the backdrop in which all businesses have to operate. Misjudging
the overall stage of the economy could jeopardize a business' profitability—and possible survival—by making unsound tactical and strategic
business decisions. This will be explored in Chapter 3. However, for business decision makers, the most important factors they need to consider
to survive and thrive are the specific *micro* circumstances affecting their
companies, such as consumers' preferences and tastes, supply chain conditions, labor availability, access to capital, and other issues that they deal
with on a day-to-day basis.

In this chapter, we will review the major explanations of the boom-
bust cycle to determine which perspective provides business decision makers with the best tools to navigate the economy's fluctuations to achieve
their strategic goals. After these perspectives are reviewed, the role of the

Federal Reserve will be analyzed. The Fed was created in 1913, ostensibly to "smooth out" the business cycle. Nevertheless, in recent decades, the Fed was given another directive by the Congress—a "dual mandate," to keep employment high and inflation low.[4] A review of the Fed's policies will reveal if the central bank is indispensable to support the economy's long-term prosperity.

John Maynard Keynes was undoubtedly the most influential economist of the 20th century. His 1936 book, *The General Theory of Employment, Interest and Money*, published during the midst of the Great Depression, purported to explain the devastating global economic downturn, which was characterized by stubbornly high unemployment and a precipitous drop in production that baffled most economists and policy makers.

The "revolutionary" theory that Keynes put forward to explain the boom-bust cycle can be summarized as follows.[5] An economy plummets when there is "inadequate demand." According to the Keynesian worldview, individual consumption, business investment, government spending, and net exports (exports minus imports from overseas) determine an economy's output. Thus, when "demand" is insufficient, both employment and production will decline. For example, less consumer spending means fewer orders for wholesalers and manufacturers that in turn reduce employment and output. And the downward cycle continues until aggregate demand is increased. Keynes believed that the boom-bust cycle is inherent in the free market and therefore market participants cannot be relied upon to spend the necessary funds to create a "full employment" economy.

This so-called market failure, which Keynes asserted is the Achilles' heel of a free market economy, leads to inadequate aggregate demand (fickle private expenditures)—and so government spending to reach full employment must prop up the economy. Keynesian economics was therefore music to the ears of policy makers who used—and have been applying—the British economist's policy prescription. Policy makers use Keynes' ideas as intellectual justification for more government spending to end a depression and thus "stabilize" the economy at or close to its full employment potential. Since the Great Depression, policy makers have enthusiastically embraced Keynes' "template" to boost economic activity when a slump has occurred.

Keynes and the New Deal

When the Great Depression began in 1929, President Herbert Hoover was in office. Historians and economists branded Hoover a "laissez-faire" president, claiming he took a hands-off approach to the deteriorating economic conditions of the country. But Hoover did in fact intervene massively to prop up production and reduce unemployment for the next three years he served in the White House. The historical record is quite clear. Hoover, in accepting his party's nomination for re-election in 1932 stated:

> we (sic) might have done nothing. That would have been utter ruin. Instead, we met the situation with proposals to private business and to Congress of the most gigantic program of economic defense and counterattack ever involved in the history of the Republic. We put it into action.[6]

What exactly were Herbert Hoover's policies to combat the economic downturn, which eventually became known as the Great Depression? Most came right out of the Keynesian playbook even before the publication of *The General Theory*. Hoover increased government spending, propping up wage rates to boost workers' incomes and offering subsidies to farmers and businesses. But Hoover's other interventionist policies—such as higher taxes and tariffs—actually discouraged consumption and production and reduced world trade. Hoover's policies like higher taxes and tariffs were not part of the Keynesian template, and had an effect opposite to what Hoover wanted. Instead of boosting the depressed sectors of the economy, Hoover's policies hindered the economic recovery.[7]

Keynesian Economics and the Federal Reserve

For the Keynesian model to be implemented, government spending should increase during the bust phase of the business cycle to take up the slack of a weakening economy. During this phase of the cycle, consumers reduce their spending for durable goods, and business investment typically plunges. As economic activity slows down, tax revenue will decline as well. The national government therefore will run budget deficits to boost aggregate demand. Given the slowdown in the economy, individuals and businesses could use some of their savings to purchase government debt as a "safe haven," which in effect will shift purchasing power from the private sector to the public sector. However, Keynesians believe the Federal Reserve should lower interest rates markedly as the economy is declining and also to boost private sector spending. Lower interest rates, according to the Keynesians, would provide a greater incentive for consumers to buy houses, automobiles, and other "big ticket" items and to spur businesses to invest in plant and equipment to rev up production.

The Fed lowers interest rates by injecting new liquidity, a (polite) technical term for creating money out of thin air, which initially enters the financial system through the banking system. The stage is set, so goes the theory, for an economic revival.

Problems With Keynesianism

There is no shortage of books, monographs, essays, and other commentaries critical of Keynesian economics. Journalist and prolific author Henry Hazlitt wrote one of the most comprehensive books dissecting Keynes' *General Theory* chapter by chapter, and he titled his critique *The Failure of the "New Economics."* In the Introduction, Hazlitt sums up the fundamental flaw in Keynes' *General Theory*, "what is original in the book is not true; and what is true is not original."[8] The basis for Hazlitt's sweeping condemnation of Keynesian economics essentially focuses on Keynes' assertion that wages and prices and therefore employment and production must be guided by government policies to achieve full employment. In other words, according to Keynes, free markets do not achieve optimal economic activity because wages and prices are "rigid" and do not adjust rapidly to changing economic conditions. Hence the government must use fiscal and monetary policies to help create jobs especially during a prolonged slump with public works programs and other expenditures.[9]

Needless to say, both Hoover and President Franklin Delano Roosevelt (FDR) used Keynesian policies once the economic downturn began in 1929 and continued throughout the 1930s. The bottom line was that the Depression lasted more than a decade even after massive monetary and fiscal stimulus and new business and financial regulations, and widespread subsidies failed to create sustainable prosperity for the U.S. economy. Despite the failure of Keynesian economic policies to lift the

U.S. economy out of the doldrums, policy makers were undeterred after World War II. Since 1945, economic downturns were not left to correct on their own but various degrees of Keynesian monetary and fiscal policies have been applied.

Critics of Keynes have pointed out that his policies would inevitably lead to more and more government spending to prop up the economy, greater doses of "easy money" to keep interest rates down, and the long-term decline of the dollar's purchasing power.[10]

Probably the most obvious flaw in Keynes' theory of the boom-bust cycle is that he does not identify a causal factor or factors that lead to a decline in aggregate demand. Why should aggregate demand decline at all out of the blue and precipitate a depression or recession? Keynes does not have an answer. His "theory" is, in the final analysis, not a theory at all but a laundry list of recommendations for policy makers to follow—primarily to increase government spending and lower interest rates by printing money—to revive the economy toward full employment.

Keynesianism and Business Planning

Can Keynesian economics help guide business decision makers during each phase of the boom-bust cycle? The short answer is no. Business planning requires entrepreneurial insight about future trends that may affect sales and expenses and therefore profitability. During the boom phase of the cycle, sales for many sectors of the economy—housing, autos, appliances, and so on are robust. Entrepreneurs, being eternal optimists, tend to expand the productive capacity to what they believe will be higher sales in the future. In addition, the commodities sector's—consisting of copper, lumber, iron, and other initial inputs into the production process—productive capacity tends to expand as well. Thus, the boom phase of the cycle is when widespread optimism creates a euphoric period of increasing sales, plentiful jobs, and a surging stock market.

Given this backdrop during the boom, why does the bust occur? Why should aggregate demand suddenly decline precipitously? What is the monetarist explanation?

Milton Friedman (1912–2006), a longtime University of Chicago economist and Nobel Laureate (1976), in his 1963 treatise with coauthor

Anna Schwartz, *A Monetary History of United States, 1867–1960*, primarily developed the monetarist school of thought to explain how money is an important factor in understanding an economy's performance, especially price inflation. The essence of Friedman's monetarism perspective is "inflation is always and everywhere a monetary phenomenon."[11] Friedman pointed out that the growth of the money supply correlates strongly with the growth in nominal income over the long term; the growth of the money supply has a short-run impact on an economy's output and later, on prices; when the money supply contracts, a depression is inevitable; and interest rates decline when money supply growth is rapid and as inflation accelerates, interest rates rise.[12]

The goal of monetarism, as expressed by Friedman, is for the central bank—in the United States, the Federal Reserve—to increase the money supply at a rate equal to the growth of real gross domestic product (GDP) in order to keep the price level stable. Thus, the economy would not experience price inflation or deflation. For Friedman, his thesis is succinct: the economy fluctuates because the central bank does not follow a monetarist rule for growing the money supply at a steady rate. In short, the business cycle *occurs* because of "the dance of the dollar" which destabilizes the economy.

Monetarism and the Economy

When price inflation accelerated in the late 1970s, President Jimmy Carter appointed Paul Volcker chairman of the Federal Reserve in 1979 to tackle the problem. The money supply had been growing at double-digit rates under Volcker's predecessor G. William Miller, and the price inflation that followed seemed to confirm Friedman's observation that prices will rise, with a lag, after the money supply grew well above the rate needed to keep prices stable.

Volcker's "tight money supply" policy paid dividends as the rate of inflation plummeted from the late 1970s to the early 1980s (see Figure 2.2). The cost of the "disinflation" was the steepest recession since the Great Depression, at least as measured by the spike in the unemployment rate in the late 1980s (see Figure 2.3). Although the two gray areas highlight the economy's back-to-back bust phase of the business cycle,

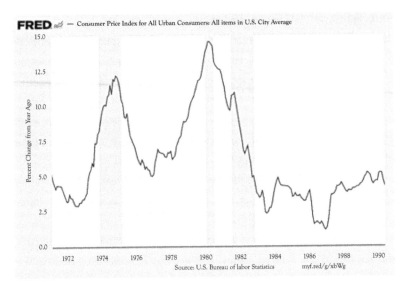

Figure 2.2 U.S. rate of inflation, 1972–1990

Source: U.S. Bureau of Labor Statistics, Consumer Price Index for All Urban Consumers: All Items in U.S. City Average [CPIAUCSL], retrieved from FRED, Federal Reserve Bank of St. Louis; https://fred.stlouisfed.org/series/CPIAUCSL, October 30, 2020.

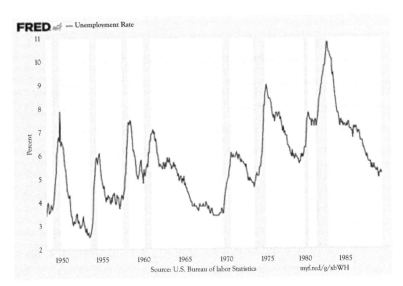

Figure 2.3 U.S. unemployment rate, 1950–1990

Source: U.S. Bureau of Labor Statistics, Unemployment Rate [UNRATE], retrieved from FRED, Federal Reserve Bank of St. Louis; https://fred.stlouisfed.org/series/UNRATE, October 29, 2020.

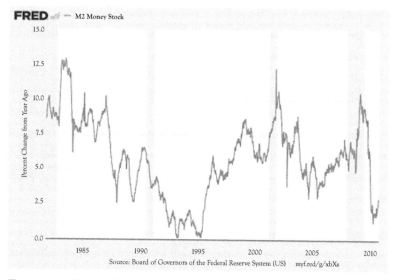

Figure 2.4 New M2 money stock

Source: Board of Governors of the Federal Reserve System (U.S.), M2 money stock [M2SL], retrieved from FRED, Federal Reserve Bank of St. Louis; https://fred.stlouisfed.org/series/M2SL, March 24, 2021.

a compelling case could be made that one long recession instead of two occurred between 1980 and 1982.

Although Friedman's monetary theory seemed to be embraced by policy makers during this period to break the back of inflation, Volcker and his successors have allowed money supply growth as measured by M2, a broad definition of money to grow erratically[13] (see Figure 2.4). Thus, to be fair, Freidman's monetarist prescription to keep the economy growing with stable prices has not been implemented.[14]

Problems With Monetarism

According to Friedman, an economy's output "depends on real factors: the enterprise, ingenuity, and industry of the people; the extent of thrift; the structure of industry and government; the relations among nations; and so on."[15] In other words, inventions, innovations, savings and investment, and international trade will create prosperity. These are fundamental economic truths. However, monetarism does not have a business cycle theory and Friedman did not develop one in his many decades as an economist and prolific author. His focus, however, on a monetary policy that would keep the price level "stable" is inconsistent with his general support of free markets. For to keep prices, in general, stable, when the tendency for prices in a free market is to slowly fall as output increases, means a central bank has to keep injecting money into the economy to prop up naturally falling prices.[16] In fact, the Federal Reserve's easy monetary policies of the 1920s kept price indexes flat but ignited stock market and real estate booms that ended when the Federal Reserve became concerned about the overheating economy and tightened money and credit in 1929 which coincided with the peak in stock market that fall.[17]

Although monetarists are correct in identifying money growth as the cause of inflation, they do not have a coherent theory of the boom-bust cycle to explain why the boom ends in a bust except to acknowledge that a reduction in money growth triggers an economic downturn.

Monetarism and Business Planning

According to Milton Friedman and other monetarists, as long as money growth is slow and steady, economic growth should be sustainable and inflation would be in check. But as the Federal Reserve chart on money growth shows (see Figure 2.4), the money supply as measured by M2 has been fluctuating—in some years erratically—for the past four decades since Volcker broke the back of inflation. Yet economic growth has occurred and so has the boom-bust cycle, which the monetarists are at a loss to explain except to decry the Fed's unsteady money creation.

Monetarism, which was implemented to some degree in the 1920s—stable prices and robust economic growth—crashed the economy by 1929. By 1929, the stock market bubble, which undoubtedly created enormous profits for investors who were able to exit before the crash, left a trail of financial destruction for those who were not fortunate enough to sell their holdings in an era of "irrational exuberance." For businesses that expanded their factories and made other capital investments, the economic downturn turned into a Great Depression caused widespread bankruptcies and unprecedented unemployment.

Even if business decision makers agree that the fundamental truth of monetarism that inflation is always a monetary phenomenon is correct, what tactics and strategies can they pursue to survive and thrive during the boom-bust cycle? Monetarism is in effect a macro approach to economic analysis and business conditions; therefore it looks at the forest instead of the trees, which would be the specific supply-and-demand conditions affecting companies' sales, expenses, and profitability. In short, both Keynesian and monetarist macroeconomic analysis do not provide business decision makers with insights they in fact have at their fingertips before the data collectors gather sufficient evidence on the state of the economy.

Supply-Side Economics

A fundamental truism of supply-side economics is that production leads to higher living standards. As long as entrepreneurs have the freedom to invest, the increase in the output of goods and services consumers will benefit in innumerable ways as we have seen in Chapter 1. In addition, supply siders assert production is discouraged when high marginal tax rates create disincentives for entrepreneurs. Furthermore, high marginal tax rates discourage both production and work, thus reducing the "optimal" tax revenue governments need to carry out their spending plans.[20]

Supply siders cite three episodes when marginal tax rates were reduced and were followed by robust economic activity. They include the Coolidge–Mellon tax cuts of the 1920s, the Kennedy tax cuts of the 1960s, and the Reagan tax cuts of the 1980s. In each instance, the economy was recovering from a depression, as was the case in the early 1920s, a mild recession in 1960, and the lengthy recession of the late 1970s and early 1980s. Supply siders argue that lowering the marginal tax rates provided substantial incentives for businesses to invest, which created multi-year booms in each decade.

According to supply siders, the Reagan tax cuts were particularly successful, because the lowering of marginal tax rates unleashed an economic boom that would not have been possible with the continuation of a high tax rates. The lower marginal tax rates on the top 10 percent of upper income owners boosted the taxes they paid to the federal government while the vast majority of taxpayers (90 percent) paid less taxes overall during the 1980s.[18]

As far as the business cycle is concerned, supply siders do not have a coherent, comprehensive theory of what causes the boom-bust cycle. According to one of the architects of supply-side economics Jude Wanniski, economic downturns are primarily caused by high tax rates.[19]

Problems With Supply-Side Economics

Critics of supply-side economics point out lower marginal tax rates did not provide a boost to business investment during the 1980s.[20] Using several metrics, the analysts concluded that supply-side policies were not a boon to business productivity, economic growth, employment opportunities, and workers' incomes. The critics assert that other forces are at work that affect economic activity besides lower marginal tax rates.[21]

Supply siders consider themselves advocates of free markets and fiscal conservatism. Yet President Ronald Reagan's economic program, "Reaganomics," which was the embodiment of supply-side policies, achieved virtually none of its objectives in the eight years of Reagan's presidency.[22] Reagan's administration policies were based on a combination of supply-side tax cuts, the promise of lower government spending and balanced budgets, deregulation, free trade, and lip service to a gold standard to prevent inflation. According to Rothbard's analysis, Reaganomics was in effect a "conservative" Keynesian economic package as opposed to the traditional Keynesian policies enacted under Democratic administrations. Deficits increased substantially as government spending outpaced any tax revenue benefits from the supply-side tax cuts. And other taxes increased, most notably Social Security taxes, to keep the Trust fund solvent. In sum, both Keynesians and supply siders support the Federal Reserve's "easy money" policies.

Supply-Side Economics and Business Planning

By focusing on the macro economy, supply siders assert that lower marginal tax rates, deregulation, open trade, and other free-market initiatives will generate robust economic activity. However, the supply-side agenda of the 1980s was in effect discarded and replaced by "big government" policies and another round of easy money policies.

For business decision makers and small business owners, lower marginal tax rates are a signal that better economic times should be ahead, especially if the economy is coming out of a recession. That is one of the biggest takeaways of the 1980s supply-side tax cuts. In addition, every recession is relatively unique as is every recovery. Nevertheless, lower tax rates do create incentives for more business investment and consumer spending. The question for entrepreneurs is: how strong will a recovery be in light of supply-side tax cuts? This is virtually impossible to forecast. But entrepreneurs are better able to judge future demand for their goods and services as another economic recovery is underway. Whether a recovery is sustainable remains one of the key concerns for all entrepreneurs.

The U.S. economy, although it is an engine of prosperity, also experiences periodic boom-bust cycles. That requires that entrepreneurs to be more nimble than they otherwise would need to be to meet consumer needs. The striking similarities between supply-side economics, Keynesianism, and monetarism cannot be dismissed or overlooked. All three schools of thought focus their attention on government policies to spur economic activity and ignore or dismiss the impact of the Federal Reserve's manipulation of money and credit that triggers the boom-bust cycle.

The next section on the Austrian school will spotlight how the business cycle unfolds and how that knowledge could be useful in both tactical and strategic planning.

The Austrian Theory and History of the Business Cycle

Throughout human history there have been periods of economic decline, which were readily understood by historians, economists, and other social scientists. A natural disaster such as an earthquake or hurricane could devastate a community or region. Wars, whether regional conflicts or a global conflagration, would cause massive destruction of property and untold deaths among the civilian population. A monarch would confiscate the people's money, usually gold or other money commodity, and would plunge the country into a depression. And crop failures would cause a precipitous drop in the public's living standards. After a short or prolonged period of depressed economic conditions because of the above factors, a recovery would occur and "normal" activity would resume.

A business cycle, on the other hand, a boom followed by a bust, is a relatively new phenomenon in the history of civilization, and the earliest systematic fluctuations coincided with the rise of the Industrial Revolution.[23] According to Austrian economist Ludwig von Mises, business cycles are not inherent in the free market. In the modern era, business cycles are caused by central banks creating "new money," which then flows into the commercial banking system.[24] The commercial banks then inflate the amount of credit—at lower interest rates—available to businesses that use the new money to purchase additional capital goods—plant and equipment, and so forth. This sets into motion the boom phase of the business cycle. Entrepreneurs see lower interest rates as a signal that the supply of savings has increased and thus embark on more time-consuming projects such as mines, factories, and so on that tend to have substantial profitable prospects. With more demand for these goods and services, prices in various sectors tend to rise—commodities, commercial real estate, and so forth—and wages tend to increase for labor needed to expand the projects that now are started that otherwise would not have been undertaken. In addition, the stock market, which represents the capitalized values of businesses, booms as well.

According to the Austrian school of economists, the boom signifies *malinvestments*, because the new projects do not reflect the amount of actual savings in the economy. In other words, in a free market, the amount of "real" savings is a reflection of the public's "time preferences." The lower the time preferences, the more savings is available and hence more investment can occur, because the public has made funds available for entrepreneurs to build and expand their businesses.

While the boom appears to be a period of robust economic activity, it in effect lays the seeds for the bust phase of the business cycle. The boom phase of the cycle creates "overheated" economic conditions, such as consumer and producers' goods price inflation, rising wage rates, speculative commercial real estate activity, and unsustainable stock market prices. A central bank will stop its expansion of new money or slow it down substantially, thus triggering a readjustment in the economy, including temporary unemployment and bankruptcies. Thus, the bust phase of the cycle, according to the Austrian theory, is inevitable after a period of monetary and credit inflation; the bust therefore paves the way for a more sustainable economy if the central bank does not intervene again. However, the central bank typically intervenes again by injecting new money to prop up the economy's distorted "structure of production," thereby preventing economic activity to reflect the actual supply and demand of both consumers and producers. Another business cycle begins.

Mises, and several of his students, most notably F.A. Hayek, Nobel Laureate (1974) for his contribution to our understanding of business cycles, and Murray Rothbard, who outlined the "Misesian" theory in numerous books, monographs, and essays have elaborated and applied business cycle analysis for the past century. The aforementioned brief summary of the Austrian theory of the business cycle reveals why a boom-bust occurs and reoccurs. For Austrian school economists, it is not a matter of looking at the "data" but of having a comprehensive explanation of the effects of so-called easy money. Other schools of thought do not believe easy money distorts the economy's real output.

Applying the Austrian Business Cycle Theory

During the worldwide boom of the 1920s Mises was warning that the world's major economies were experiencing unsustainable business conditions and that a bust would occur. At that time, Mises was director of an economic research organization in Vienna, Austria, where he collaborated with his student F.A. Hayek. When the boom ended in the U.S. 1929 stock market crash that fall Mises' forecast was vindicated. Two years later Hayek gave several lectures in London explaining the Austrian school theory of the business cycle. Young economist began to embrace the Mises–Hayek explanation of the boom-bust cycle and its remedy—namely, central banks should no longer inflate, and governments should not try to prop up the economy with spending and other interventionist policies. However, the publication of Keynes' *General Theory* in 1936 shunted aside the Austrian school's explanation of the boom-bust cycle and policy prescriptions for free markets in favor of more inflating, deficit spending and more regulations. The Keynesian revolution was underway.

Unfazed, Mises barely escaped from his native Austria with his wife after the German army marched in and he immigrated to the United

States in 1940. He became a visiting professor at New York University and resurrected his famous Vienna seminar for aspiring young economists in lower Manhattan. One of the students, Murray Rothbard, applied the Mises theory of the business cycle to explain America's first Great Depression, the subject of his doctoral dissertation at Columbia University, which was published as *The Panic of 1819* in 1962. A year later Rothbard's explanation of the events leading to the stock market crash of 1929 and the early years of the Great Depression was published, *America's Great Depression*.

Austrian economists have applied the Austrian theory to explain the stagflation of the 1970s, the dot-com bubble, and the housing bubble in the most recent "everything bubble."[25] The Austrian school does have its detractors, including Stefan Erik Oppers, who wrote the International Monetary Fund (IMF) working paper, "The Austrian Theory of Business Cycles: Old Lessons for Modern Economic Policy?" In his criticism of the Austrian business cycle explanation, Oppers makes a typical critique, namely that "its proponents have presented little direct quantitative research to support their cycle theory."[26] Austrian economists deny that empirical evidence can prove the validity of an economic theory—unlike data, which are essential to prove or disprove a theory in the so-called hard sciences.[27] Economic events are the result of a multitude of factors, which coalesce to create outcomes in the business world. Suffice it to say, Austrian economists do not deny empirical data are important, but data are useful to illustrate how an economy is affected by specific monetary, taxation, spending and regulatory policies. In others words, data cannot be used to develop a theory nor verify one.[28]

The Austrian School and Business Planning

According to the Austrian theory of the business cycle substantial profits can be made during the boom phase. However, these profits can easily turn into losses if entrepreneurs have miscalculated the demand for their products because easy money during the boom has misdirected resources throughout the economy and particularly their sector. For "nimble" entrepreneurs, the boom phase of the economy poses a challenge: namely how long will the boom last, and how deep will be the bust? These are unknowns. Nevertheless, there are several tactics and strategies business owners and corporate managers could pursue to navigate the economy's booms and busts.

For the owner of a mom-and-pop shop, business—and profitability—appears to be endless during the boom. This would be a time to build up cash reserves for a future downturn. However, it is tempting to expand the size of the store, if possible, or open another location. This would be prudent if the economy was on a noninflationary and sustainable path. The major concern would be consumer demand. In other words, are there changing tastes, preferences, demographics, and other factors, which would cause sales to decline? A SWOT analysis, therefore, would be helpful for a small business owner to meet future business conditions.

Insofar as we live in a boom-bust cycle world, what actions should a small business owner take to survive and thrive after a severe or mild bust? We know that the purchase of discretionary consumer items are typically postponed during an economic downturn—housing, autos, jewelry, clothing, appliances, and so forth that would then constitute pent-up demand during the next upswing in the economy. Businesses that sell nondiscretionary items—food and other frequently consumed household items—tend to do well during each phase of the business cycle. Nevertheless, a prudent increase in cash reserves is warranted given the uncertainties of the next downturn. Cash is a valuable asset just like inventory, equipment, and other items. A cash "hoard" could then be used during the downturn to pick up inventory or other assets for your business at a deep discount.

A severe downturn in which unemployment skyrockets like the 1930s had a substantial impact on many mom-and-pop businesses. And in the spring of 2020, during the pandemic lockdowns, unemployment skyrocketed but the laid-off workers saw their incomes initially propped up by the federal government stimulus checks allowing consumers to continue purchasing nondiscretionary items. In short, both state unemployment benefits and federal government spending cushioned the lockdowns during the first half of 2020. However, many small businesses were adversely affected by lockdown such as restaurants, movie theaters, and other businesses that depend on substantial traffic. E-commerce boomed as consumers shifted their spending to online sites, video streaming services, and other businesses that either expanded or initiated an online presence.

Clearly, unanticipated events such as COVID-19 and the subsequent lockdowns revealed how financially unprepared small businesses were to ride out the draconian policies. Cash therefore becomes an important asset for small business owners to meet a future unprecedented challenge.

For publicly held companies, the boom phase of the cycle usually brings record profits, much higher stock prices and the temptation to expand their operations, take over or merge with competitors, or enter new lines of businesses. One tactic a public real estate company could use during the boom phase, for example, is to build a mall, a skyscraper, a hotel, or other asset and sell it to a competitor. However, if the company wants to hold the new project in its portfolio, it must be aware that when the downturn occurs, there may be a cash flow squeeze and thus the projected profits may not materialize. A company, therefore, could buy a "put" on the property, that is, an option to sell it at a fixed price after a specific period of time to a potential buyer. This would allow the company to protect itself if the market for commercial real estate weakens. If the boom continues and the property appreciates, then the company would not exercise the put.

Publicly held companies also should build up a prudent cash position during the boom to weather any future downturn. This cash position could be extremely valuable during the next downturn to purchase deep discounted assets or whole companies or parts of companies that would make a good strategic fit. Major U.S. companies led by Apple, Microsoft, and Berkshire Hathaway have an enormous amount of cash on their balance sheets as of March 2020.[29]

In the next chapter, we will explore how to identify the end of the boom and the bottom of the bust so business decision makers can improve their companies' performances during each phase of the business cycle. In the meantime, the last section of this chapter will explore how the Federal Reserve's policies have played a role in the business cycle.

The Role of the Federal Reserve

President Woodrow Wilson signed the Federal Reserve Act in December 1913. The Act was the culmination of several years of discussion—beginning with a secret meeting on Jekyll Island off the coast of Georgia with a few Wall Street bankers and key Congressional leaders—within the

Congress and members of the banking community about how to create a central bank, which would be charged to prevent financial panics and stabilize the economy. Over the years, Congress has expanded the Federal Reserve's mandates such as the Full Employment Act of 1946 "to promote maximum employment, production, and purchasing power"; the Full Employment and Balanced Growth Act of 1978 added price stability and promoted long-term growth to the Fed's mandate.[30]

Since the Fed began operations a year later, both critics and proponents of central banking have made their views known in endless number of speeches, books, essays, and monographs.[31] Critics of the Fed cite the Fed's inflating of money and credit during World War I, which preceded the so-called forgotten depression of 1920–1921 and the subsequent easy money policies of the Roaring Twenties that culminated with the stock market peak in the fall of 1929 and the economy's readjustment to the inflated real estate and other sectors that benefited from the easy money policies during the decade. President Hoover's interventionist policies unfortunately prevented the necessary adjustment of wages and prices, which would have sped up the conditions to generate a sustainable recovery in the 1930s.[32] Instead, the Fed intervened again by lowering interest rates to prop up the economy and federal spending and taxes increased, which put additional burden on the private sector delaying a recovery. A decade-long depression thus ensued.

The federal funds rate is the target interest rate set by the Federal Reserve Open Market Committee (FOMC) at which commercial banks borrow and lend their excess reserves to each other.

In the post–World War II era the Federal Reserve manipulated the fed funds rate, to inject new money in the economy and withdraw funds from the banking system. As Figure 2.5 reveals, the fed funds rate has been anything but stable over the past six decades and thus confirms what Austrian school economists have asserted: namely that the Fed destabilizes the economy by "manipulating" short-term interest rates. The boom-bust cycle therefore is not inherent in the market economy but instead is a consequence of the Federal Reserve intervening in the short-term money markets ostensibly to stabilize the economy and promote economic growth and full employment.

The economic and financial data do not support the assertion that the Federal Reserve has been able to "stabilize" the economy since it was

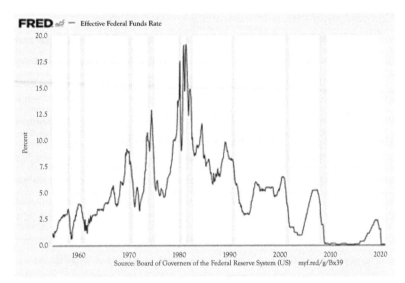

Figure 2.5 Effective federal funds rate over the past six decades

Source: Board of Governors of the Federal Reserve System (U.S.), Effective federal funds rate [FEDFUNDS], retrieved from FRED, Federal Reserve Bank of St. Louis; https://fred.stlouisfed.org/series/FEDFUNDS, March 24, 2021.

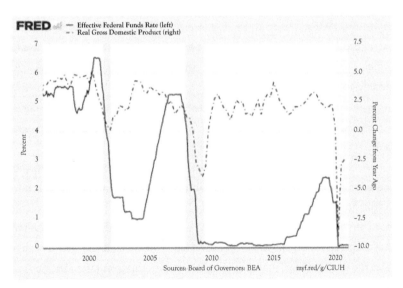

Figure 2.6 Fed fund rate and real gross domestic product (1998–2020)

Source: U.S. Bureau of Economic Analysis, Real Gross Domestic Product [A191RL1Q225SBEA], retrieved from FRED, Federal Reserve Bank of St. Louis; https://fred.stlouisfed.org/series/A191RL1Q225SBEA, November 03, 2020.
Board of Governors of the Federal Reserve System (US), Effective Federal Funds Rate [FEDFUNDS], retrieved from FRED, Federal Reserve Bank of St. Louis; https://fred.stlouisfed.org/series/FEDFUNDS, November 03, 2020.

created. In fact, since the Fed was created, the United States experienced the worst depression in its history that lasted a full decade, and in recent years has created three back-to-back bubbles by dropping interest rates to lower and lower levels (see Figure 2.6), revealing the U.S. economy has become dependent on more and more debt—and financial boosts—to generate economic growth.[33]

Bubble Problems for Business

According to the Austrian school, the boom-bust cycle will be with us as long as the Federal Reserve continues to manipulate interest rates to achieve its economic and financial mandates. Corporate decision makers and small business owners thus need to keep their eyes on the two balls, the fundamentals of their businesses and the monetary policies that impact the supply-demand factors that in turn affect their revenue, expenses, and therefore profitability. Because the fundamentals and the business cycle are intertwined, decision makers need to determine how much of their business is sustainable and how much of its sales are subject to business cycle dynamics. Being able to distill the economy's overall trajectory would help businesses make the best decisions possible to survive and thrive during the cycle.

So how should business decision makers manage their enterprises in a boom-bust economy? They could take the advice of one of the most successful money managers. Peter Lynch who headed up the Fidelity Contrafund stated, "I've always said if you spend 13 minutes a year in economics, you wasted 10 minutes." Even if Lynch is correct, the time you spend understanding where the economy is in the business cycle will give you an edge in managing your corporation or small business. The discussion above reveals why applying the insights of the Austrian school explanation of the business cycle is the most valuable tool for business managers and small business owners.

The next chapter will help business decision makers pinpoint when the boom phase of the cycle is ending and when the next upturn will begin in our mixed economy.

CHAPTER 3

How to Identify the End of the Boom and the Bottom of the Bust

The United States has multiple economies. We have an economy based upon production, savings and investment, and ultimately consumption. This is the economy most people understand because they participate in it as a corporate executive or manager, small business owner, employee, and, of course, consumer. Businesses have one primary goal, to satisfy consumer demands. And the market economy has been "delivering the goods" to the American people for more than 200 years. In addition, we have a substantial portion of the economy, the so-called public sector, which requires taxes and borrowing to spend on transfer payments—Social Security, Medicare, Medicaid, and other social welfare programs. The federal government also spends hundreds of billions of dollars on national defense and other military and security items. Lastly, the federal government spends hundreds of billions of dollars on so-called discretionary spending and interest on the national debt. Altogether in fiscal year 2020, because of the extraordinary expenditures during the Covid epidemic, the federal government spent $7 trillion and incurred a deficit of $3 trillion. Moreover, the Federal Reserve "enables" the federal government to spend by buying some of the debt, known as monetizing the debt, which creates money out of thin air.

The focus of this chapter is, how do identify the end of the boom and the bottom of the bust. In other words, we're talking about the high and low cycle points of the cyclical economy that is a mystery to most Americans. People know there are good times and there are bad times but they really do not understand why there are bad times. The previous chapter concluded with the observation that the Federal Reserve's easy money policies initiate an unsustainable boom, which inevitably leads to a bust.[1] The material that follows will *illustrate and highlight* several key economic and financial factors that will reveal when the unsustainable boom ends and when the next cycle begins.

We will refer to various charts published by the Federal Reserve Bank of St. Louis and the links to them, which highlight the discussion to follow. These charts reveal the effects of easy money policies on the real economy, and we will present three indicators that corporate managers and small business owners should monitor closely to prepare for an economic downturn.

Employment

The U.S. economy has been a job-creating machine for the past eight decades. In addition, employment tends to plateau as the economy reaches its business cycle peak and then declines when employees are laid off in the industries that were "overextended" during the boom.

During the boom, the unemployment rate declines reflecting not only the long-term demand for labor in new companies and industries but also the demand for labor in the industries benefiting from the decline in interest rates such as finance and real estate. The unemployment rate begins to decline usually as the recession is ending or a few months afterward. Unemployment rate *skyrocketed during the 2020 pandemic lockdown* and subsequently declined as businesses were allowed to reopen. This was not a typical cyclical unemployment phenomenon that has occurred in previous decades. However, the decline in the unemployment rate to 3.2 percent early in 2020 was comparable to previous end of boom phases of the cycle. In other words, the long boom since the Great Recession (2008) was nearing its end, but the pandemic lockdowns accelerated the rise in unemployment for a brief period until governors began to open up their economies.

The trend of manufacturing employment in the United States tells two stories. First, the long-term uptrend in manufacturing occurred from 1940 until its peak in 1980. Second, with the peak of manufacturing employment in 1980, *there has been a long-term decline* especially from 2000 onward. The question, therefore, remains: will manufacturing employment return to its glory days of four decades ago?

During the boom-bust cycle, we would expect manufacturing employment in durable goods industries to fluctuate more than nondurable goods employment, because the Federal Reserve's easy money policies, which depress interest rates make some projects attractive to business decision makers, as was explained in Chapter 2. In addition, nondurable goods employment was steady for several decades before it began its secular decline in the mid-1980s.

The interest-sensitive industries, autos, appliances, and so on fluctuate more than food, clothing, and other nondurable sectors. Motor vehicle employment, for example, has fluctuated markedly within a secular downtrend in recent decades.

The Finance and Insurance employment data reveal another sector where fluctuations during the business cycle are obvious. Employment in this sector essentially boomed for more than a decade and then peaked before the housing bubble burst in 2007–2008. The sector had a substantial contraction and then began turning up in 2010.

A similar pattern can be observed in Construction employment, which correlates with the Finance and Insurance sector. Employment was robust from the 1990s until the housing bubble burst in 2007.

Personal Income

During the boom phase of the business cycle, personal income will increase, and depending upon how much money has been created by the Federal Reserve, the rise could be substantial, for example, what happened in the inflationary decade of the 1970s. After the peak of price inflation in the early 1980s, personal income growth has decelerated for four decades. The deceleration in the growth of personal income varies during each cycle and therefore there is no hard and fast rule about how personal income can pinpoint peaks and troughs of the business cycle.

Moreover, personal income also includes transfer payments from the government, which means that even though employees in the most economically sensitive industries lose their jobs, unemployment benefits and other social welfare spending kicks in and buffers their lost income. Thus, we need to drill deeper into personal income data to see how it fluctuates with the business cycle.

The fluctuations in the compensation of employees in private industries, which are the main beneficiaries of the boom, take the brunt of the pain during the bust.

During the dot-com boom of the 1990s, compensation soared at a 10 percent annual rate of change by the late 1990s and then fell off a cliff as the recession began. During the housing bubble, compensation peaked a couple of years before the recession began and then dropped precipitously until the rate of change bottomed out in 2009. In the most recent phase of the cycle, initiated by the economic lockdown during the spring and summer of 2020, compensation in the private sector fell dramatically and then rebounded in the third quarter of 2020.

As each economic cycle is "unique," we see the lead-time of compensation in the private sector dropping, which varies from cycle to cycle. This should not be surprising because each cycle has specific circumstances that will affect all the data surrounding the boom and bust phases.

Lastly, the compensation for durable goods employees fluctuates more than that of employees in the nondurable goods manufacturing sector as expected. The most dramatic decline in durable goods sector occurred during the housing bubble as economic activity in industries allied to real estate plunged.

Profits

During the boom phase of the business cycle, profits will rise as companies generate more sales and easy money conditions put more money in the pockets of consumers. As the boom phase peters out, total profits in corporate America begins to decline as we saw in the dot-com boom of the late 1990s and the housing bubble of the mid-2000s. In addition, in the latest boom phase of the cycle, profits were strong especially after the drop in the corporate tax rate that took effect in 2018. However, profits plunged in mid-2020, as the lockdowns shut down a good portion of the economy because of the pandemic.

As expected, profitability in the machinery sector, the key capital goods industry, fluctuated widely since the dot-com bubble, the housing bubble, and the most recent boom phase of the cycle.

The construction sector saw even greater fluctuations in profitability especially during the housing bubble and bust. Subsequently, as a succession of quantitative easing—the official term for creating new money—steps by the Federal Reserve, which lowered interest rates virtually nonstop since 2008, profitability has soared in the construction sector.

The previous narrative clearly shows how easy money has had an enormous impact on the profitability of two of the most interest-rate sensitive sectors of the economy.

The Industrial Sector

Fluctuations in industrial production vary from cycle to cycle. Industrial production peaked in 2000 and bottomed out in 2001. Industrial production then had a robust uptrend during the housing bubble, picking up just as the recession began; the Great Recession pummeled industrial production during the downturn. The subsequent rebound in industrial production after the Great Recession was quite uneven and then plunged during the 2020 pandemic. Industrial production was peaking in late 2019, even before the pandemic hit the U.S. economy, suggesting the boom phase was running out of the steam before the lockdowns occurred.

Business equipment production fluctuated markedly during both the dot-com and the housing bubbles and ensuing busts. The subsequent rebound since the Great Recession has been impressive but bumpy, and it petered out for the 2020 pandemic.

The construction supply sector is another volatile component of industrial production. The long boom in this sector was interrupted by the dot-com bust, peaked as the Great Recession began, and then plunged precipitously. The robust rebound during the past decade peaked just before the pandemic of 2020 unfolded and then fell sharply and rebounded.

Consumer goods production had a long cycle, declining briefly during the dot-com bust and then peaking before the Great Recession began in 2007. The widespread impact of the Great Recession caused consumer goods production to plummet as well, revealing how a deep downturn in the economy affects all sectors including the least sensitive such as consumer goods production. The relatively muted rebound in consumer goods production since the end of the Great Recession reveals it was peaking before the pandemic of 2020 began. The quick plunge in production was followed by a sharp rebound as some of the lockdowns ended.

Although not technically considered part of industrial production, housing starts and its relationship to short-term interest rates that the Fed influences reveal the relationship that unfolds during the business cycle. From the trough in 1990 housing starts began a robust recovery until it peaked well before the housing bubble burst nearly two decades later. As the Federal Reserve lowered short-term interest rates and kept them there for a couple of years fueling the bubble, the subsequent plunge revealed the enormous speculative excesses in this sector.

Michael Lewis captures the essence of the speculative bubble in his best-selling book, *The Big Short*.[2] Other writers such as William Fleckenstein in *Greenspan's Bubbles* and David Stockman in *The Great Deformation* provide additional analyses of the Federal Reserve's easy money polices and their impact on the housing sector.[3] The most recent boom in housing again was cut short by the 2020 pandemic early in the year, and the Fed funds rate plummeted as well as after the multiyear rise, which reversed in 2019. Since the plunge in the housing sector in early 2020, robust sales accelerated as mortgage rates dropped to all-time lows.

Another clear indication of the housing bubble can be found in the median price of houses sold. Median house price increased virtually interrupted since the early 1990s until they peaked just before the housing bubble burst and the Great Recession was underway. After recovering slowly after the crash, housing prices began another upward move before peaking a couple years before the 2020 pandemic.

Retail Sales

Retail sales increase over time for obvious reasons—population growth, rising living standards, new products, and of course more money in consumers' pockets as the Fed's easy money policies diffuse through the economy. The Great Recession caused retail sales to plunge dramatically because the layoffs reduced consumer spending and retailers discounted the merchandise to move inventory off their shelves.

Heavy vehicle sales have been one of the most sensitive sectors during the business cycle. This sector reflects the boom and bust of the capital

Table 3.1 Websites for employment statistics data

Employment	https://fred.stlouisfed.org/graph/?g=wp8I
Unemployment rate	https://fred.stlouisfed.org/series/UNRATE
Manufacturing employment Durable goods employment Durable goods compensation Business equipment Industrial production	https://fred.stlouisfed.org/series/MANEMP https://fred.stlouisfed.org/series/DMANEMP https://fred.stlouisfed.org/series/PRS31006062 https://fred.stlouisfed.org/series/IPBUSEQ https://fred.stlouisfed.org/series/INDPRO
Motor vehicle employment Heavy vehicle sales	https://fred.stlouisfed.org/series/CES3133600101 https://fred.stlouisfed.org/series/HTRUCKSSAAR
Finance/Insurance employment	https://fred.stlouisfed.org/series/CES5552000001
Construction employment Construction supply sector	https://fred.stlouisfed.org/series/USCONS https://fred.stlouisfed.org/series/IPB54100S

goods industries, because heavy vehicles are used in the transportation of machinery and other interest-sensitive products. The most recent robust heavy sales period stopped on a dime just before the pandemic began.

In contrast, the sales of beer and wine consistently rise in good or bad times, and, not surprisingly, rose dramatically as tens of millions were forced to work from home during the pandemic.

Meanwhile, e-commerce sales took off during the beginning of the dot-com era and has not looked back. The 2020 lockdown gave online sales an extraordinary shot in the arm as more retailers had to shift their business model from in-store sales to online to survive.

Links to the above indicators can be found at the St. Louis Federal Reserve database, FRED.

You can view links to key economic and business indicator data in Tables 3.1 and 3.2.

Table 3.2 Websites for personal income, retail sales, housing starts, and other statistics

Personal income Personal income private sector	https://fred.stlouisfed.org/series/PI https://fred.stlouisfed.org/graph/?g=xI91
Consumer goods production	https://fred.stlouisfed.org/series/IPCONGD
Retail sales	https://fred.stlouisfed.org/series/RETAILSMSA
Housing starts	https://fred.stlouisfed.org/series/HOUST
E-commerce sales	https://fred.stlouisfed.org/series/ECOMSA
Profits	https://fred.stlouisfed.org/graph/?g=xL4T

Stock Market

A market economy needs capital—the ultimate financial resource—for businesses to increase their productive capacity, invest in R&D, purchase a competitor, expand overseas, and so on. The stock market allows relatively young companies to raise capital by going public and established companies to raise additional funds to implement their strategic plans. The market economy would not be as successful as it has been to increase living standards without the stock market that makes capital formation possible—the engine of the economy. In other words, capital formation is the key to sustainable prosperity, because it makes possible the continuous production of consumer goods and services. There are no shortcuts to creating a prosperous society. So contrary to conventional thinking that "consumption" drives the economy, without capital necessary for production to occur consumption would be at the subsistence level.

In a free market economy, the stock market in general would not have a boom-bust cycle. Instead, the stock market would increase modestly over time, reflecting the savings and investment preferences of individuals, the retained earnings of corporate managers, and other market participants such as endowment funds and pension funds. Many companies would prosper, some would have modest success and others would fall by the wayside. In general, however, profits would increase over time, reflecting the entrepreneurial expertise of corporate managers and small business owners.

The stock market cycle, moreover, reflects the Federal Reserve's monetary policies, which in effect manipulate short-term interest rates known as the federal funds rate (see Figure 3.1) as part of its "toolkit" to carry out its mandate—to maintain employment high and keep inflation low.

The stock market has had two major boom-bust cycles since the 1990s. The first one is related to the dot-com bubble, which peaked in 2000. The housing bubble peak in the S&P 500, one of the broadest stock indexes comprised of 500 companies, analysts focus on to get a pulse of the stock market, occurred in late 2007. In each case the market reached an all-time high and then plateaued for several months before declining to the bear market low a couple of years later in 2002 and 2009, respectively.

The next stock market upswing began in March 2009 and looked like it was peaking in 2015 when it exhibited the same pattern as the two

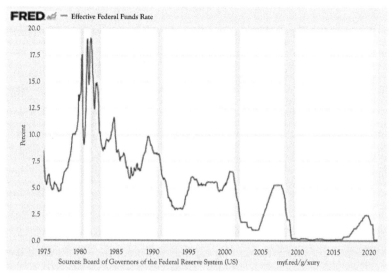

Figure 3.1 The federal funds rate

Source: Board of Governors of the Federal Reserve System (U.S.), Effective federal funds rate [FEDFUNDS], retrieved from FRED, Federal Reserve Bank of St. Louis; https://fred.stlouisfed.org/series/FEDFUNDS, November 05, 2020.

previous peaks. In retrospect, that plateau was just a basing pattern for the next leg of the bull market that, at this writing, is still underway.

Investment analyst Martin Pring points out in a blog post that his proprietary indicator (KST, which stands for Know Sure Thing) of the stock/bond ratio provides clear buy signals based on the observation that stock become more attractive to invest in than bonds during the course of a stock market cycle.[4] According to the latest trend in the indicator, a buy signal was on the horizon in late 2020.

The high-flying dot-com stocks were trading on the NASDAQ exchange in the 1990s, and the following chart shows the speculative bubble that occurred. The NASDAQ 100 index soared approximately 10 times from the 1990 low and then crashed more than 80 percent bottoming out in 2002, and then tripled to the housing bubble peak in 2007 before bottoming out after a 50 percent correction in 2009. Since the Great Recession bottom, the NASDAQ 100 has been on a tear climbing more than tenfold by late 2020.

When will the current bull market end? One indicator that waves the yellow flag that Warren Buffett keeps his eye on is the relationship between corporate equities and GDP. This indicator reached an all-time high at the dot-com bubble peak in 2000, and is currently above that level in November 2020.[5]

This indicator reached a major bottom in 1982 coinciding with the beginning of the great bull market run from that year to 2000. The chart also reveals that this indicator can increase for several years before reaching a peak with the stock market as it did in 2000. In other words, this is an indicator worth monitoring for a clue when the current bull market will end.

Investment analyst Tom McClellan shows there is an uncanny relationship between the price of oil and the stock market, namely, the price of oil foretells the stock market peak 10 years in the future (see Figure 3.2). McClellan has no explanation for this relationship but he back-tested the data and, lo and behold, it has held up for the past 100 years. The next peak in the stock market should occur in 2024—an ominous sign for the Biden presidency. Then the stock market is poised for another upswing beginning in 2026 and peaking a few years later, 100 years after the crash of 1929. As we have seen, major financial crashes have occurred in 100-year cycles, the Panic of 1819 the Forgotten Depression of 1920, and the pandemic crash of 2020.

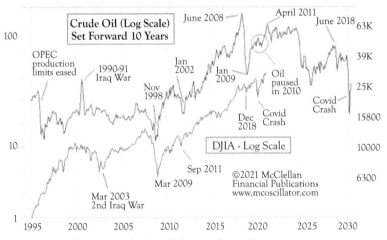

Figure 3.2 The price of oil and the stock market

Courtesy of Tom McClellan. Original chart appeared at www.mcoscillator.com, https://mcoscillator.com/learning_center/weekly_chart/crude_oils_10-year_message/

The Key Boom and Bust Indicators

In a free market economy, without a central bank manipulating interest rates, the yield curve—the interest rate for short- and long-term securities— would be relatively flat, because there would be no price inflation.[6] The yield curve, which fluctuates during the course of the boom-bust cycle, indicates, to a large degree, the effects of the Federal Reserve's manipulation of the Fed funds rate, the interest rate it targets to keep the economy humming. Thus, the yield curve is generally considered one of the best indicators signaling a coming recession and the start of the next boom.

The inverted yield curve is a leading indicator of the boom-bust cycle (Figure 3.3). The lead-time varies as the chart reveals, because each cycle affects business decision makers differently and thus the economy will unfold depending how "wide and deep" the distortions are as a result of the Federal Reserve's easy money policies. Therefore, there is no hard and fast rule we can apply regarding this indicator except that it provides corporate managers and small business owners with sufficient time to plan accordingly—raise cash, project sales for the next couple of years

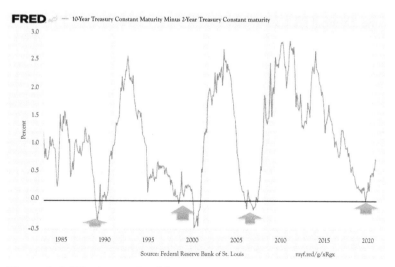

Figure 3.3 The inverted yield curve

Source: Federal Reserve Bank of St. Louis, 10-year treasury constant maturity minus 2-year treasury constant maturity [T10Y2Y], retrieved from FRED, Federal Reserve Bank of St. Louis; https://fred.stlouisfed.org/series/T10Y2Y, November 17, 2020.

using scenario analysis, the what if exercise to determine what revenue and expenses will be under several possible circumstances.

The yield curve has gone negative and then positive and then negative again, which is highlighted by the arrows before each of the past three recessions. In 2020, the yield curve briefly went negative, then the pandemic hit and the Federal Reserve lowered short-term rates virtually to zero, making the curve positive again. Thus, the next time the yield curve turns negative, the onset of the next recession probably will be unfolding.

The Fed funds rate is one of the most watched financial indicators because it is the Federal Reserve's primary tool to "manage" the economy. The Fed funds rate rises when the Fed decides to "fight" inflation and ends its easy money policies. When the Fed funds rate stops increasing, the bust is right around the corner. The Fed then reverses course as the recession unfolds and reduces the federal funds rate to "stimulate" the economy. And another boom cycle begins.

There are scores of business and financial indicators that also provide a hint of the boom-bust cycle. Suffice it to say, there is no need to be overwhelmed with data to help manage your business. In fact, a strong case can be made that business decision makers should monitor closely the trends in their sectors in conjunction with the prior financial indicators to get ahead of the business cycle curve.

CHAPTER 4

Wash, Rinse, Repeat

Does the Past Determine Our Economic Future?

For more than 200 years, the U.S. economy has been on an upward trajectory despite numerous setbacks along the way. The virtual nonstop output of goods and services has been one of the great success stories of Western civilization.

People from Europe and other continents came to America even before the republic was created in 1788 and began to build one the most dynamic economies in human history. Probably the greatest challenge the American people faced occurred 160 years ago when the union was nearly torn apart by the Civil War. The war caused, according to new estimates, more than 800,000 deaths on both sides and untold destruction and damage to factories, farms, and infrastructure throughout the young nation. The regional rivalry culminated in the abolition of slavery, which many historians cite as the cause of the South's desire to secede from the union, but other historians and economists assert the federal government's tariff policies triggered the South's desire to leave the union that they voluntarily consented to join in the previous century.[1]

Prior to the Civil War, the United States and Britain squared off in the War of 1812, which nearly derailed the new republic's quest for continued independence. Nevertheless, war inevitably brings economic pain and dislocations. The economic fallout from the War of 1812 can be traced to the battle between Alexander Hamilton, America's first treasury secretary, and Thomas Jefferson, his political and philosophical rival, over their respective visions for America's future.

Hamilton's vision was nothing less than centralization of economic power in the federal government. He favored tariffs and other taxes to generate revenue for the new republic, and paying off the Revolutionary War debt the states and the Continental Congress acquired. Hamilton also wanted the federal government to charter a national bank and create a national currency. Jefferson, on the other hand, opposed concentration of economic power in the federal government and was skeptical about banks, which he believed "encouraged speculation."[2]

Despite Jefferson's concerns and opposition, Congress soon adopted many of Hamilton's recommendations including the establishment, in 1791, of the Bank of United States and granting it a 20-year charter. One of Jefferson's main objections to the bank was his belief that the Constitution did not authorize the Congress to create one. Nevertheless, Hamilton and his supporters viewed the bank as a necessary institution to help grow the economy and also would be instrumental in eventually making United States a global economic power.[3]

The bank's 20-year charter expired prior to the War of 1812, and the Second Bank of the United States was charted in April 1816. President James Madison signed the charter even though he had been a political ally of Jefferson. Bank began operations a year later and was similar in structure to the First Bank. The second bank held federal deposits and issued debt, supervised state chartered banks, and accepted deposits to make loans to individuals and businesses within its 25-bank network.[4]

The Panic of 1819

Soon after the bank began its operations in 1817, the U.S. economy experienced its first depression, the Panic of 1819. The genesis of America's first (great) depression, according to a synopsis of what is considered a definitive account of the panic, Murray Rothbard's *The Panic of 1819*, the War of 1812 led to a "boom" financed by the creation of paper money by state banks to finance the conflict. At the time, banks were required to "back" their notes with specie (typically gold and silver), and when the supply of notes increased markedly, many banks suspended redeeming their notes, beginning in 1814. Without specie redemption, the number of banks proliferated, primarily outside of New England, as did the amount of paper money in the economy. The inevitable price inflation and boom followed.[5]

As Rothbard explains, the Panic of 1819 mystified most observers at the time who could not understand why the so-called good times lead to a huge bust. The boom had a huge impact on trade with Europe. Although exports increased substantially, imports increased more rapidly. In addition,

> The rise in export values and the monetary and credit expansion led to a boom in urban and rural real estate prices, speculation in the purchase of public lands, and rapidly growing indebtedness by farmers for projected improvements. The prosperity of the farmers led to prosperity in the cities and towns—so largely devoted were they to import and export trade with the farm population.[6]

As the boom unfolded, a new institution was created in 1817, the New York Stock Exchange. Instead of trading on the curbs of Wall Street, traders now moved indoors. This period also saw the beginning of investment banking. Needless to say, although the foundation of America's financial system was being shaped, the banking sector spearheaded by the Second Bank of United States and its expansionary policies sowed the seeds of the boom-bust cycle, which was baffling to policy makers and the general population. As confidence in banks declined because they issued more notes than specie on deposit, the public began to redeem as many of their notes as possible, causing the banks to be in a more precarious financial situation. The Second Bank of United States then began the painful contraction of notes in circulation in the summer of 1818. As supply of money declined and liquidity became a problem for many sectors of the economy, the Panic of 1819 soon followed. The deflation that occurred was is in effect the necessary period of adjustment to reduce the inflated prices during the unsustainable boom after the War of 1812.[7]

Although the economy began to recover in 1821, urban unemployment had increased substantially as manufacturing workers, most of whom were self-employed, bore the brunt of the depression. Individuals who had borrowed heavily to speculate in land and other ventures caused bankruptcies to skyrocket.[8] In short, the Panic of 1819—the first recognizable boom and bust cycle—had all the characteristics of future business cycles in the 19th century. As Rothbard explains,

The period also saw much of the typical characteristics of later financial panics: expansion of bank notes; followed by a specie drain from the banks both abroad and at home; and finally a crisis with a contraction of bank notes, runs on banks, and bank failures. A corollary to the contraction of loans and bank runs was the scramble for a cash position and rapid rise in interest rates during the panic.[9]

Reoccurring Panics

The Panic of 1819 thus provided a glimpse of what was to come during the remainder of the 19th century. Major banking panics occurred in 1837, 1873, 1884, and 1893.[10] As the 19th century unfolded, America was transformed from an agricultural, rural based society into an urban, industrialized economy by the beginning of the 20th century. According to David Erickson, "This enormous social change and the increasing complexity of economy arguably exacerbated the consequences of the financial panics and other economic disruptions in later periods."[11]

Rothbard, however, paints a more optimistic picture of the second half of the 19th century. He points out that the U.S. economy was working on all cylinders as production and real output per capita increased markedly from 1879 to 1896. The year 1879 saw a return to the gold standard, which was suspended during the Civil War. Rothbard points out that the gold standard gave more stability to the financial system and banking sector. He also questions whether there was a great depression from 1873 to 1879, which orthodox economic historians have asserted was a period of depressed economic conditions.[12] Although prices fell during this period, production increased confounding economists who believe that price deflation is associated with depressed economic conditions.

In the meantime, the National Banking Act of 1863, 1864, and 1865 created a quasi-central bank centered on Wall Street, which allowed the banking system to "inflate the supply of notes and deposits in a coordinated manner." Nevertheless, as the economy was growing up especially in the heartland, St. Louis and Chicago became important banking centers, and the major complaint of the big Wall Street banks was that there was a need for the money supply to be more "elastic," which is a euphemism for the ability to expand money and credit.[13]

The Panic of 1893 ignited a populist movement headed by William Jennings Bryan, who became the Democratic Party's nominee for president in 1896. Bryan's anti-gold convention speech ignited a political firestorm and led to realignment of American politics. The pro gold Democrats threw their support behind the Republican presidential nominee William McKinley who was elected with strong backing from the Wall Street banks. The Wall Street bankers then pressed for financial "reforms," namely, an "elastic" gold-based monetary system, which would allow the banks to inflate in a concerted manner without igniting a financial panic.[14]

The Gold Standard Act was passed in March 1900 and put the United States on a single gold standard, with silver fulfilling a minor role in the monetary system. The debate, therefore, of having a bimetallic monetary system was basically laid to rest. This contentious issue sparked passionate political conflicts throughout most of the 19th century, but as gold won out for the time being, the unfolding of America's financial and banking system continued.

Panic of 1907

Before the end of the first decade of the 20th century, another panic gripped the nation. According to Moen and Tallman, the role of trust companies, primarily located in New York City, is considered the focal point of the panic. As state-chartered institutions, trust companies accepted deposits in competition with banks and kept only around 5 percent reserves relative to their deposits while national banks maintained a 25 percent reserve ratio.[15] In other words, trust companies were susceptible to runs if their customers lost confidence in them. In addition, trust companies provided loans to New York Stock Exchange brokers, which typically had to be repaid at the end of the day.[16]

In October 1907, two speculators failed in their attempt ("cornering the market") to make a killing in a mining stock, United Copper. As a word of their failure made the rounds on Wall Street, depositors began to run on the banks associated with their speculation. A few days later, the New York Clearing House calmed the situation and the bank run was halted, but not before a run began on the trust companies, especially Knickerbocker Trust, triggering a major financial crisis in the New York City. Initially, J.P.

Morgan decided not to aid the trust companies but eventually changed his mind. Nevertheless, depositors continued to withdraw funds from the trust companies and interest rates spiked as there was a scramble for short-term funds, and only after the New York Clearing House injected liquidity into the financial system did the panic subside.[17]

The economic fallout from the panic caused industrial production to fall by 17 percent in 1908 and real GNP contracted by 12 percent. The good news was that the economy recovered in a little over a year.[18]

In their conclusion about the Panic of 1907, Moen and Tallman observe:

> The panic of 1907 took place over 100 years ago, before the establishment of the Federal Reserve System, the Federal Deposit Insurance Corporation, or the Securities and Exchange Commission—institutions designed to bring stability to banking and financial markets. Before these institutions, the National Banking Act provided the regulatory structure of guarding the day-to-day behavior of banks, particularly the largest and most interconnected ones. During the panic, however, the acts provided little guidance to bankers coping with large-scale withdrawal of deposits.[19]

The Panic of 1907 was the impetus to create a central bank that would be in the final analysis a lender of last resort to bail out shaky banks.[20] In order to get the general public to support a government-sponsored central bank when distrust of Wall Street and banks was widespread, the financial elites came up with an elaborate plan to sell the public the idea of having a bank that would "stabilize" the financial sector. What emerged from this effort eventually turned out to be the Federal Reserve.

Creation of the Federal Reserve

At a secret meeting (November 1910) at the Jekyll Island Club, off the coast of Georgia, the blueprint for the Federal Reserve was ironed out by six men, a powerful Republican senator, Nelson A. Aldrich from Rhode Island, representatives from major Wall Street banks, and a member of the recently created National Monetary Commission, whose task was to pave the way for the public and the banking community to support a central bank.[21]

The creation of the Federal Reserve essentially capped the end of the Progressive Movement in America, which supposedly was a period of "reform" to break up monopolies with antitrust legislation, expand democracy with the direct election of senators (17th Amendment), and put a check on corporate power with the creation of such agencies as the Federal Trade Commission (FTC) and the Food and Drug Administration (FDA) among others. The reality, according to some historians and other social scientists, is that the progressive movement was in effect a means to expand the economic power of certain business interests at the expense of the public. Inasmuch as cartels are unsustainable in the free market, business interests sought the power of government to achieve their goals.[22]

After a three-year campaign to gather both public and congressional support, President Woodrow Wilson signed the Federal Reserve Act on December 23, 1913. America's bankers finally got a central bank whose mission was to be a lender of last resort, smooth out the business cycle, and maintain the purchasing power of the dollar. All worthy goals to be sure. But as Rothbard concludes after extensive research in the history of the Fed's creation,

> The financial elites of this country, notably the Morgan, Rockefeller, and Kuhn, Loeb interests, were responsible for putting through the Federal Reserve System, as a governmentally created and sanctioned cartel device to enable the nation's banks to inflate the money supply in a coordinated fashion, without suffering a quick retribution from depositors or noteholders demanding cash.[23]

The Federal Reserve opened its doors in 1914. Despite having substantial tools at its disposal to achieve its three initial goals—maintain the purchasing power of the dollar, smooth out the business cycle and be a lender of resort for the banking system—the business cycle has not been "smoothed out," the dollar's purchasing power has fallen by 95 percent since 1914, and the financial system has been bailed out on numerous occasions, most notably during the Great Recession of 2007–2009. In short, why has the business cycle not been banished or at least tamed, as the proponents of central banking have asserted it would be if the United States adopted an institution with broad regulatory and other powers to shore up the banking system?

Recurring Cycles

The same year the Federal Reserve began operations (1914), the Great War—now known as World War I—erupted in Europe. The belligerent nations resorted to higher taxes and borrowing and printing money to pay for the armaments each side needed to conduct the war. President Woodrow Wilson ran for the 1916 election with a promise to keep Americans out of the war. After he was reelected and a month after his inauguration, Wilson declared war (April 1917) on Germany and her allies.[24]

The U.S. economy was booming during the Great War, supplying foodstuffs and other materials to the European powers. When the United States entered the war, taxes were raised substantially, especially on upper income earners who saw their marginal tax rate reach 77 percent. The federal government also borrowed substantial sums from the public to fight the war. Buying liberty bonds was considered an essential patriot act. In addition, the Federal Reserve provided considerable liquidity to the banking system. The U.S. economy was in the boom phase of the business cycle. Even after hostilities ended in 1918, many analysts predicted a major correction that did not materialize. Instead, the economy was in full throttle and price inflation was accelerating. However, when it comes to the business cycle, what goes up must come down.

The Federal Reserve's easy money policies generated exhilaration in virtually all sectors of the economy.[25] From raw materials to autos and other consumer goods to farm products, rising prices created substantial profits for companies and the farming community. Soon, however, the boom turned to bust beginning in early 1920. The unemployment rate zoomed from 4 percent to nearly 12 percent and the economy contracted 17 percent. With President Wilson debilitated by a stroke in his last year in office, the federal government did not try to "stimulate" the economy to bring down unemployment and boost the output of goods and services.

The election of Warren G. Harding (1920) and his response to the unfolding depression, according to James Grant, was the last time the federal government did not intervene in economy with fiscal stimulus to boost the economy. In addition, instead of lowering interest rates to stimulate production, the Federal Reserve raised rates.[26] The 18-month depression, as painful as it was, was the last *laissez-faire* response to the bust phase of the business cycle. Both wages and prices fell, and sure enough, when prices became attractive for employers and investors, they began to spend and invest to end the correction that was inevitable after the unsustainable boom generated by the easy money policies of prior years.

Interestingly, the Federal Reserve's history page makes no mention of the 1920–1921 depression, which is quite surprising since the portal provides substantial information about previous and subsequent boom-bust cycles. Could it be that one reason the Federal Reserve is reluctant to present information about the "forgotten depression" is that it does not fit the narrative that a laissez-faire approach to economic downturns is the best way to end the bust phase of the business cycle?[27]

Nevertheless, the U.S. economy recovered during the 1920s, a period dubbed the Roaring Twenties, as the introduction of new products and technologies such as radio and other home appliances stimulated both production and consumption. Auto sales reached a feverish pitch as the mass production of motor vehicles made them more affordable to many households. However, the Federal Reserve was not "hands off" during the decade. It injected substantial liquidity in the banking system that created a boom in both stocks and real estate throughout the decade.[28] The real estate bubble burst in 1926 and the famous stock market peak of September 1929, when the Dow Jones Industrial Average reached 381.22, was followed by a nearly 90 percent decline over the next several years to 41.22 in July 1932 (see Figure 4.1). After the 1932 bottom, stock market roared ahead until it reached another peak in 1937 (see Figure 4.2).

Although the 1930s has been recognized as the Great Depression conventional dating of booms and busts recognize the early period of the depression, as a major downturn was followed by a "boom" and then another downturn in the middle of the decade, and then an economic expansion until the end of World War II as measured by industrial

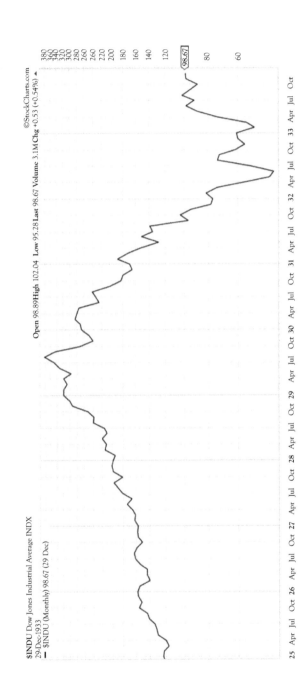

Figure 4.1 The stock market crash, 1929–1932

Chart courtesy of stockcharts.com

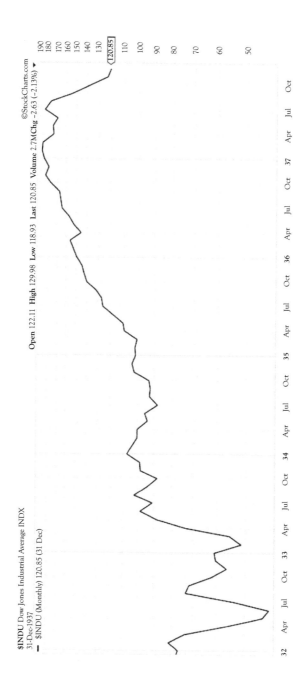

Figure 4.2 The stock market boom, 1932–1937

Chart courtesy of stockcharts.com

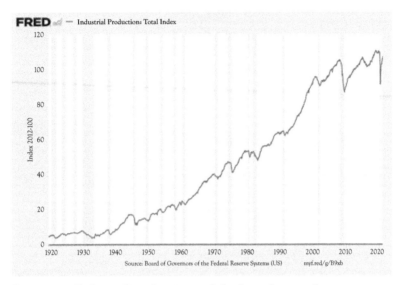

Figure 4.3 Industrial production and the boom-bust cycle

Source: Board of Governors of the Federal Reserve System (U.S.), Industrial production: Total index [INDPRO], retrieved from FRED, Federal Reserve Bank of St. Louis; https://fred.stlouisfed. org/series/INDPRO, March 10, 2021.

production (see Figure 4.3). Unemployment was still in double digits throughout the decade. At the eve of World War II, the unemployment rate was between 10 and 15 percent, hardly a period of prosperity, but then declined as the postwar boom kicked in as pent-up demand helped ignite the prosperity of the 1950s and 1960s, which was interrupted by several recessions (Figure 4.4).

Clearly, in the U.S. economy, there has been a major uptrend since the "washout" of the 1929–1932 stock market decline and Great Contraction. For all intents and purposes, the stock market has been on a long-term uptrend since the end of World War II. Nevertheless, there have been multiyear secular booms (1949–1966 and 1982–2000) and multiyear periods of secular stagnation (1966–1982 and 2000–2014, Figure 4.5). Within the long-term trends, there were "cyclical" market booms and busts when severe declines were followed by sharp rallies. Even the record one-day decline (22.6 percent) in October 1987 is a "blip" in the long-term bull market that began in August 1982. Currently, it appears we are in another secular bull market. How long it will last remains to be seen. If history is any guide, it could last until the end of the 2020s.

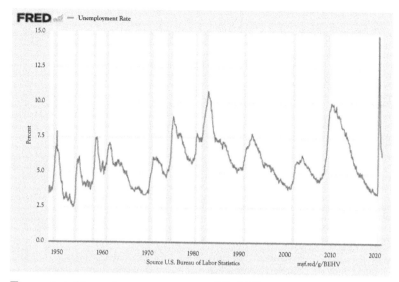

Figure 4.4 *Unemployment rate since World War II*

Source: U.S. Bureau of Labor Statistics, Unemployment rate [UNRATE], retrieved from FRED, Federal Reserve Bank of St. Louis; https://fred.stlouisfed.org/series/UNRATE, March 10, 2021.

However, it would not be surprising if the stock market has several sharp cyclical declines from now until the end of the decade, which occurs during every secular bull market.

Annual real GDP growth has been positive except for the recessions during the past 75 years. The boom phase of the business cycle occurs as "natural" economic forces kick in. In addition, rather than allowing the recovery to occur on a sound footing, real savings, and market interest rates, the federal government "primes the pump" with deficit spending and the Federal Reserve opens the money spigot to give the economy additional "oomph" to boost the economy. These have been the twin policies since the Great Depression.

Prior to the millennium, on many occasions, the economy grew at a 5 percent or more for several quarters during the boom phase of the cycle. Since 2000, an interesting cyclical phenomenon has occurred. There has not been one quarter of real GDP exceeding a 5 percent annual growth rate. There have been many explanations put forward as to why the U.S. economy is mired in relatively tepid economic growth since the end of the dot-com bubble. One that is consistent with the Austrian school business

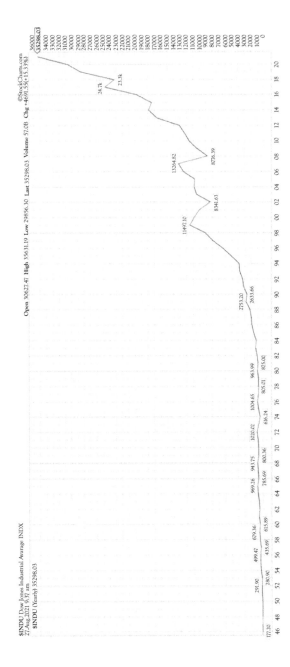

Figure 4.5 Long-term market cycles

Chart courtesy of stockcharts.com

cycle theory, namely, that after the dot-com bubble burst, the Federal Reserve lowered interest rates to nearly 1 percent in the early 2000s, then to nearly zero again after the Great Recession (2007–2009), and most recently during the 2020 pandemic with the injections of liquidity. These ultra-easy money episodes primarily boosted asset values. The easy money episodes of the past two decades, instead of "stimulating" the economy's output of goods and services have impeded the "price discovery" necessary to create a robust economy, and that is why real savings, not money printing, are the key to sustainable prosperity.[29]

Does a 100-Year Super Cycle Determine Our Future?

The U.S. economy has had several major panics, depressions, and economic contractions since the birth of the country. Is there a pattern to all these major downturns in the economy? For example, the Panic of 1819 was America's first Great Depression. Hundred years later, roughly speaking, the forgotten depression of 1920 began. Coincidence? The Panic of 1873, which ended the speculation after the Civil War in which there was enormous overinvestment in the railroads, preceded the first oil crisis in 1973 by a 100 years and ushered in the deepest recession at that time since the Great Depression.

The Panic of 1907, which provided the impetus for the creation of the Federal Reserve a few years later, occurred 100 years before the great recession of 2007–2009. The forgotten the depression of 1920–1921 occurred 100 years before the pandemic of 2020. In 2020, the stock market had its one-month decline in February to March and the market rebounded sharply after the Federal Reserve flooded the financial system with new money.

The next 100-year super cycle date, the stock market crash that began in the fall of 1929, implies that a major financial event could occur around 2029. Although there is no theoretical foundation for these 100-year cycles, they are nevertheless real. Whether a crash in 2029 occurs remains to be seen, but if a crash does happen at the end of this decade, then economists, financial historians, and others will have a fertile area for research to explain how major financial cycles have occurred almost like clockwork every 100 years.

Irrational Exuberance: Avoidable or Inevitable?

In their classic *Manias, Panics, and Crashes*, Robert Z. Aliber and Charles P. Kindleberger identify 10 bubbles beginning with the Dutch tulip mania in 1636 and ending with the real estate bubble in United States and other European nations. In between, the authors cite the U.S. stock market bubble of the late 1920s and the dot-com bubble in the late 1990s as classic bubble episodes.[30] The authors point out that, "Manias—especially macro manias—are associated with economic euphoria; business firms become increasingly upbeat and investment spending surges *because credit is plentiful*[31] (emphasis added). In Japan, Real estate prices and stock prices headed to the stratosphere as bankers made credit easily available. With an enormous amount of liquidity in their country, "the Japanese purchased 10,000 items of French art."[32]

The authors acknowledge what previous analysts have identified as the cause of bubbles and manias. "Speculative manias gather speed through expansion of credit. Most increases in the supply of credit did not lead to a mania—but nearly every mania has been associated with rapid growth in the supply of credit to a particular group of borrowers. In the last 100 years, the increases and supplies of credit have been provided in part by the banks, in part by the development of new financial instruments and in part by cross-border investment inflows."[33]

More often than not "frauds and swindles" have been occurring with get-rich-quick schemes such as the infamous Charles Ponzi, who in the 1920s promised investors 45 percent interest, and for 18 months, he kept his "Ponzi" game going until there was no money there for depositors to withdraw funds. Most recently, Bernie Madoff's Ponzi scheme, estimated to be as high as $64 billion, collapsed in December 2008 just as the real estate bubble was bursting.[34]

These two notorious episodes reveal how slick financial salesmen promising extraordinary returns can dupe investors as in the case of Charles Ponzi or in the case of Bernie Madoff who promised investors relatively risk-free steady rates of returns. In both instances, investors obviously did not do their due diligence, relying instead on the trustworthiness and credibility of both Ponzi and Madoff. In short, investors who got in late lost most or all of their money.

But what about "honest" bubbles that create "irrational exuberance" in the financial world? The term became popular after Alan Greenspan delivered a speech in December 1996 when he was chairman of the Federal Reserve, indicating that the stock market may have reached frosty levels. Yale economics professor Robert Shiller in his best-selling book, *Irrational Exuberance*, published at the height of the dot-com bubble in 2000, pointed out that the economy suffered a form of psychological dysfunction, which causes investors to throw caution to the wind and thus invest unwisely to obtain abnormal profits.

> I define speculative bubble as a situation in which news of price increases spurs investor enthusiasm, which spreads by psychological contagion from person-to-person, and, in the process, amplify stories that might justify the price increase and brings in a larger and larger class investors, who, despite doubts about the real value of the investment, are drawn to it partly through envy of others' successes and partly through a gambler's excitement.[35]

Financial analyst Frank Shostak takes issue with Shiller's diagnosis of bubbles and points out that he only describes a bubble's characteristics without focusing in on the underlying cause(s) of what objective factors precipitate a bubble in the first place. According to Shostak, a "monetary balloon" causes ballooning asset prices, that is, an expansion of the money supply, which he asserts is similar to "counterfeiter" that diverts resources from the creation of a real wealth to nonproductive activities.[36] For Shostak then, psychology is irrelevant in understanding bubbles; an analyst should focus on the growth of the money supply which sets into motion the unsustainable booms in various sectors of the economy, typically the stock market and real estate. In addition, he points out that as the rate of growth of the money supply declines, the bursting of the bubble inevitably follows.

As long as the money supply keeps growing, the bubble can inflate, which according to Fleckenstein and Sheehan gets a boost in part by the financial networks reporting of the substantial run-up in various stock sectors. The financial networks thus play a role in igniting additional investor interest in high-flying stocks. So as the bubble unfolds, it tends to feed on itself.[37]

At the end of 2020, there is a difference of opinion among financial analyst whether the current stock market recovery from the pandemic low of March 2020 is another of irrational exuberance.

Former Reagan's budget official David Stockman has asserted that the stock market is out of touch with reality. Former CNBC anchor Ron Insana makes the case that many of the same factors that were evident in previous bubbles are obvious in 2020, such as "extreme day-trading, and the unprecedented gains in mega stocks coupled with rapid speculation in so-called penny stocks."[38]

CHAPTER 5

Managing the Supply Chain

Even if business cycles never existed, managing a business successfully is challenging. These challenges include competition, changing consumer preferences, input price pressures, selling prices, cash flow issues, employee morale, strikes, taxes, regulations, geopolitical events, natural disasters, quality control, and of course supply chain disruptions. In other words, entrepreneurs should be thinking of value networks that will allow them to switch out links, take new routes from supplier to market, and be agile and flexible. Business is a constant swirling flow of change and more change.[1] And in 2020, COVID-19 caused the greatest challenge to American businesses—large and small—possibly in our country's history as many states and cities locked down "nonessential" businesses for weeks or months and then imposed draconian restrictions as they slowly allowed restaurants, gyms, hair salons, and small shops to reopen. During 2020, 29 retailers declared bankruptcy, including such iconic retailers such as JCPenney, Lord & Taylor, Neiman Marcus, and Brooks Brothers.[2] And thousands of small businesses have closed their doors permanently.

And during the 2007–2009 Great Recession, retailers that filed for bankruptcy or liquidated their businesses included, Chrysler, GM, KB Toys, Circuit City, CompUSA, Linens 'N Things, Fortunoff, Levitz, and Bombay, while other retail outlets reduced the number of brick-and-mortar stores.[3]

A successful business where "all cylinders" are working smoothly will no doubt be profitable and sustainable. If one or more of a business' cylinders is underperforming, then the enterprise could not only suffer losses but its survival could also be in jeopardy. The business cycle, however, adds another dimension that poses a huge challenge to managing a business. Just when it appears that a company is firing on all cylinders, the bump in the road—a major economic decline (the bust phase of the cycle)—could turn profits into losses and could jeopardize a business' very survival.

Thus, the U.S. economy is in reality multidimensional. We have the "real" economy based upon savings, investment, consumer preferences, and international trade; in other words, the voluntary choices of buyers and sellers that create the economy's mosaic of goods and services valued by consumers. Imposed on the economy is the business cycle, which we have seen is "man-made" and manifests itself in distorting the structure of production leading to unsustainable booms and painful busts. Consequently, the supply chain would be affected from raw materials to consumer sales during the business cycle. An overview, therefore, of the business cycle and the supply chain would provide managers with insights on how to best manage their enterprises no matter where their business is in the structure of production.

One template of viewing the economy is based on Sean Corrigan's cone of production (see Figure 5.1).[4] Over time, primary (raw) materials, mixed with capital become intermediate goods, which are then distributed to wholesalers and eventually to consumers. Essentially, this is the flow of goods in the free market economy. In short, we can trace the roots of every consumer good back to its "state of nature" and then follow its journey as these raw materials are eventually transformed into retail products that are purchased in stores or online. In other words, virtually all the

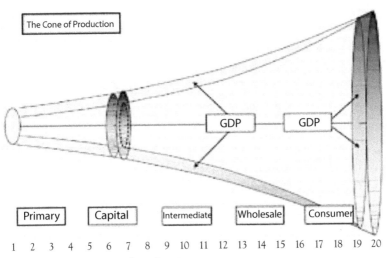

Figure 5.1 The cone of production

Source: Sean Corrigan's "Cone of Production," https://mises.org/library/cone-production

challenges cited at the beginning of the chapter must be addressed continuously for all firms to be profitable. Inasmuch as in a growing market economy, profits are more prevalent than losses, and the entrepreneurs/ managers who are the most adept in organizing their businesses will be the most successful.

All final sales comprise the nation's GDP. A major shortcoming of GDP is that it fails to capture the enormous business-to-business (B2B) transactions throughout all stages of production before products reach the consumer.[5] B2B sales comprise all the economic activity throughout the "structure of production"—the stages through which goods flow from raw materials to eventually becoming consumer goods. For example, the production of a pencil, a "low tech" product, requires billions of dollars of investment in forests, saw mills, petrochemical plants, mining, rubber plantations, transportation equipment, and so on.[6] In other words, the "stuff" necessary to make a consumer product requires an extensive array— and co-ordination—of goods and services to bring a simple good as a pencil to retailers. The pencil supply chain is thus global and far-reaching.

Our task here is more "micro" oriented, namely, how managers can recognize an impending economic downturn in order to avoid suffering losses to stay afloat and thrive. By avoiding losses, or at least keeping them to a minimum, a business can come out of recession in a much better position than when the economy rolled over.

The cone of production, which is synonymous with the structure of production, and is a proxy for the supply chain. How is the supply chain affected during the business cycle? Supply chain management and business cycles were the subject of a research note by Heng et al. in 2005.[7] The authors cite the work of economists, other academics, and practitioners who focused their attention on inventory fluctuations as the driving force generating business cycles. The so-called acceleration principle is thus responsible for the business cycle; namely, a burst of investment in inventory and capital goods leads to excessive inventories and thus trigger an eventual downturn in the economy.[8] Although the role of monetary policy as the transmission mechanism for the business cycle is acknowledged, the authors cite the work of Ramey who concludes that demand for inventory is foremost in understanding the business cycle.[9] In other words, the proponents of the acceleration principle *describe* where the distortions in the economy primarily occur and disregard the monetary factors, that is, easy money policies of the Federal Reserve, which set into motion the "excesses" that unfold during the business cycle.

Timing the end of the boom and the beginning of the subsequent recession is always fraught with error. If managers are too cautious during the boom, they will miss out on potential profits. On the other hand, if they were too optimistic as the boom unfolds and expand their capacity and production, the ensuing recession would reveal the errors they made. So what should managers do in general during the course of the business cycle?

One of the most common phenomena during the upswing in the business cycle especially in the later stages is that prices begin to rise as the Fed's monetary inflation that began during the recession to stimulate the economy diffuses throughout the structure of production and provides the fuel for entrepreneurs to raise prices. This poses a particular challenge to managers, namely how much of these rising costs can be passed on to the next stage in the cone of production without losing sales or reducing the quality of their output to keep prices in check. Another factor to deal with is higher labor costs as employers scramble to find qualified employees to fill new positions or replace workers who have left because of retirement or have found other positions. Several strategies to deal with higher inflation include "building strong supplier relationships, inventory management, identifying demand forecasts of products/services, identify long-term production strategies and reaching out to both upstream and downstream suppliers among others."[10] Managers should assess what strategies to pursue depending on a company's position in the cone of production and which specific approaches to pursue to dampen the impact of inflation on the business' output and inputs.

At the end of 2020, commodity prices were on an upswing after a decline in the previous two years. The collapse in price of crude oil by more than two-thirds from 2014 to 2016 had a major impact on the commodity index. The uptrend in the price of crude oil at the end of 2020 was then a major factor in the overall commodity price index rising at that time. How long this trend continues remains to be seen during this cycle. In the meantime what will be the impacts on the supply chain will have to be assessed by managers if they do not take pre-emptive actions, as a commodity boom is underway to avoid the "squeeze" of higher input prices. In short, higher input prices can erode profit margins markedly and thus cause issues with suppliers who are also trying to maintain their margins.[11]

Raw Materials

Just as commerce is the lifeblood of civilization, raw materials are the lifeblood of the supply chain and the production process. From copper, lumber, iron ore, crude oil, rare earth minerals, and dozens of other commodities, which must be extracted from the earth, the producers of raw materials as well as the consumers of the resources that nature provides must work harmoniously for the supply chain to operate smoothly. Suppliers of raw materials are subject to environmental regulations, volatile prices, labor strikes, competitive pressures, domestic and global logistical challenges, and of course the business cycle. In other words, the challenges facing raw material producers are formidable. Nevertheless, without raw materials, civilization ceases to exist, as we know it.

Raw materials can be divided into two categories—direct materials, which is self-explanatory, and indirect materials, the supplies necessary to bring the raw materials to the marketplace.[12] All direct and indirect materials, therefore, must be part of the planning process to calculate the costs of production. In addition, "in many cases, while it is always better to calculate than to predict, materials planning may include forecasting due to seasonality, market volatility or *other external factors*" (emphasis added).[13] One of the primary external factors is the business cycle, which has a profound impact on the raw materials supply chain.

With the supply chain having gone global the past several decades, factors such as lead time, mode of production, long/short supply chain legs, overstocking and understocking, and quality and compliance issues all weigh on managers' ability to optimize the raw materials supply chain.[14]

One of the greatest challenges that face raw materials managers is relying on optimistic forecasts, which would cause overstocking of several commodities such as copper, lumber, and crude oil, to name a few. For example, the price of copper (see Figure 5.2), one of the most price-sensitive raw materials that fluctuates markedly during the business cycle, poses an obvious challenge to producers, namely, when to expand capacity, how much to put into inventory, how much to discount as demand falls, when to close mines as demand slows, and so on.

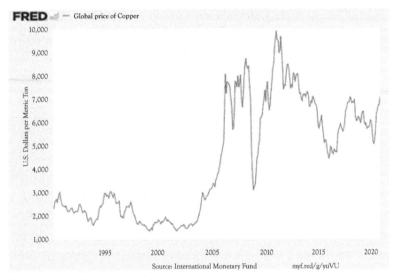

Figure 5.2 Global price of copper

Source: International Monetary Fund, Global price of Copper [PCOPPUSDM], retrieved from FRED, Federal Reserve Bank of St. Louis; https://fred.stlouisfed.org/series/PCOPPUSDM, December 11, 2020.

The same concerns apply to lumber, where production is highly correlated with housing starts, a key indicator of the business cycle (see Figure 5.3). Although the correlation is not "perfect," the volatility in lumber prices reflects how this commodity is affected by factors other than just housing starts and the business cycle (recessions are shaded gray).

U.S. Census Bureau and U.S. Department of Housing and Urban Development, Housing starts: Total: New privately owned housing units started [HOUST], retrieved from FRED, Federal Reserve Bank of St. Louis; https://fred.stlouisfed.org/series/HOUST, December 21, 2020.

Lastly, the price of crude oil (see Figure 5.4) has had a history of widespread volatility since the first oil crisis in 1973–1974 and then again in the late 1970s. The collapse in all prices in the mid-1980s and then the spike a few years later wreaked havoc with the economies of such cities as Houston, which is at the epicenter of the oil trade in the United States. Commercial real estate was overbuilt in Houston and the subsequent collapse in prices (mid-1980s) and then again in the early 1990s created enormous opportunities for investors who had the cash or the ability to borrow from the banks to purchase real estate properties

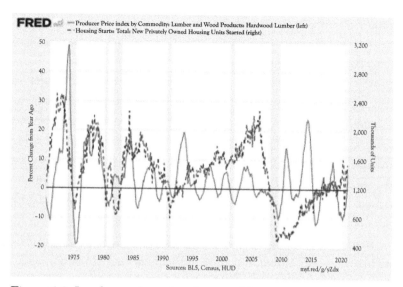

Figure 5.3 Lumber and wood products and housing starts

Source: U.S. Bureau of Labor Statistics, Producer price index by commodity: Lumber and wood products: Hardwood lumber [WPU0812], retrieved from FRED, Federal Reserve Bank of St. Louis; https://fred.stlouisfed.org/series/WPU0812, December 21, 2020.

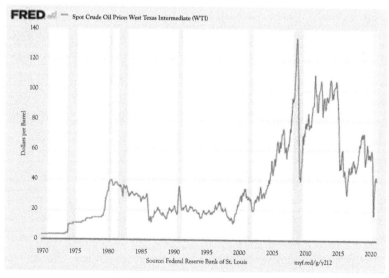

Figure 5.4 Spot crude oil price: West Texas Intermediate

Source: Federal Reserve Bank of St. Louis, Spot crude oil price: West Texas Intermediate (WTI) [WTISPLC], retrieved from FRED, Federal Reserve Bank of St. Louis; https://fred.stlouisfed.org/series/WTISPLC, December 20, 2020

and/or oil properties at depressed prices.[15] And since the end of the dot-com bubble in the early 2000s, the price of oil has been on amazing roller coaster for the past two decades.

With the push for electric cars throughout the world, the question remains whether the price of crude oil will be permanently repressed, or if another bout of price inflation in the 2020s will lift crude oil prices and other commodities well above their current levels. And another variable that could impact the price of oil would be any new initiatives to reduce the use of hydrocarbons in the coming decades from the Biden administration. Thus, oil producers will be hard-pressed to forecast an accurate price of oil for the remainder of the decade.

A sustained rise in commodity prices, however, is a real possibility based on the enormous increase in the money supply during 2020. According to several analysts, the "money pump" to counter the effects of the COVID-19 lockdowns will boost prices in general and commodity prices in particular.[16] Previous commodity booms were preceded by easy money policies in the United States and around the world.[17]

The bottom line for managing raw materials and the supply chain is to be flexible and nimble, especially as the business cycle unfolds over time. Several tactics should be pursued for both material producers and raw material users. Raw material suppliers should monitor economic conditions as closely as possible and avoid overstocking their inventory. Insofar as an inverted yield curve is a precursor to a recession—and the cable business channels report on this phenomenon frequently—the lead time before a recession begins should give managers ample time to decide if the "big one" is coming—a downturn that could cause a precipitous drop in commodity prices.

For users of raw materials, having several suppliers during the boom is important to avoid any production bottlenecks. Relying on one or even two suppliers during the boom when commodity prices are typically rising could have a negative impact on the bottom line if prices of a company's output cannot be raised to cover its cost hikes. One way to avoid prospective price hikes during the boom is to make pre-emptive purchases. The danger here is increasing inventories of several commodities could backfire if a recession occurs soon thereafter when commodity prices may be falling. Thus, purchasing agents must try to gauge strength of the boom and forecast when the downturn may occur to minimize the negative impact of rising and falling commodity prices.

Intermediate Products

In the supply chain, intermediate products are in effect a way station to eventually reaching the consumer. Intermediate products can be characterized as durable and nondurable goods. Durable goods would include wood products, nonmetallic mineral products, primary metals, machinery, computer and electronic goods, motor vehicles and parts, among others. Nondurable goods would include relatively recession-proof products such as food, beverages, and tobacco and more economically sensitive products such as textile and product mills, paper, apparel and leather, petroleum and coal products, chemicals, and plastic and rubber products. These products are thus processed to satisfy consumers' demands, both durable and nondurable goods, which will be reviewed in the next section.

During the business cycle, we would expect durable manufacturing, one of the most economically sensitive sectors, to fluctuate more than the nondurable manufacturing sector. Over the course of many cycles since the mid-1970s, durable manufacturing rose faster during booms and fell greater in the bust than the less-sensitive nondurable manufacturing sector. The drop in manufacturing during 2020 was not your typical business cycle plunge and recovery. However, Figure 5.5 reveals that manufacturing was beginning to slow down during 2019, before the pandemic lockdown pushed manufacturing over the cliff. In other words, a typical cyclical slowdown was unfolding as in previous cycles with nondurable goods contracting faster this time than durable goods manufacturing.

As far as intermediate goods prices are concerned during the business cycle, Figure 5.6 highlights the gyrations since the first oil shock recession of 1973–1975. Intermediate goods prices tend to decelerate prior to the start of a recession and occasionally decline year-over-year. The sharpest decline occurred during the housing bust of 2007–2009 when petroleum products prices plunged, driving the index into negative year over year change (see Figure 5.7).

For intermediate goods producers, the challenges during the business cycle are as follows. During the boom phase, as raw material prices

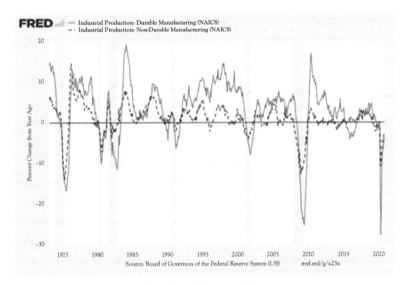

Figure 5.5 Durable and nondurable manufacturing

Source: Board of Governors of the Federal Reserve System (US), Industrial Production: Durable Manufacturing (NAICS) [IPDMAN], retrieved from FRED, Federal Reserve Bank of St. Louis; https://fred.stlouisfed.org/series/IPDMAN, December 22, 2020.
Board of Governors of the Federal Reserve System (US), Industrial Production: Non-Durable Manufacturing (NAICS) [IPNMAN], retrieved from FRED, Federal Reserve Bank of St. Louis; https://fred.stlouisfed.org/series/IPNMAN, December 22, 2020.

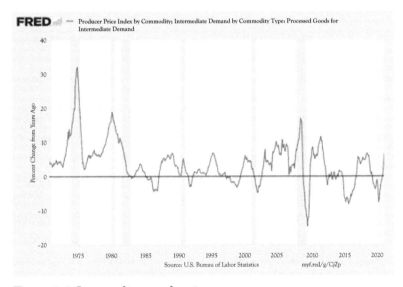

Figure 5.6 Intermediate goods prices

Source: U.S. Bureau of Labor Statistics, Producer price index by commodity: Intermediate demand by commodity type: Processed goods for intermediate demand [WPSID61], retrieved from FRED, Federal Reserve Bank of St. Louis; https://fred.stlouisfed.org/series/WPSID61, March 25, 2021.

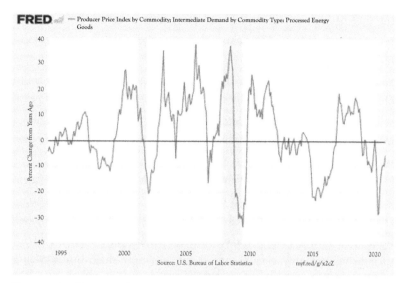

Figure 5.7 Processed energy goods prices

Source: U.S. Bureau of Labor Statistics, Producer Price Index by Commodity: Intermediate Demand by Commodity Type: Processed Energy Goods [WPSID69113], retrieved from FRED, Federal Reserve Bank of St. Louis; https://fred.stlouisfed.org/series/WPSID69113, December 22, 2020.

are increasing a company's margins may be squeezed if it cannot pass its higher input costs on to wholesalers and/or retailers. Depending upon the industry of the intermediate goods supplier, resistance to higher prices in the early stages of the boom may be significant. However, as the boom unfolds, wholesalers and retailers may be more willing to pay higher prices because the injections of new liquidity that kick-started the boom may be sufficient for them to pay the higher prices and pass on higher prices to consumers. For example, the price of inputs to computer manufacturing may be increasing, and if the final demand for computers is also robust, then computer manufacturers should have no problem raising prices.

When the boom reaches a peak, intermediate goods manufacturers may be in a major price squeeze as raw materials may still be rising but the final demand is flattening or beginning to decline. And if intermediate goods manufacturers have overestimated final demand, they may have inventories piling up just as final demand prices are falling.

Retail Supply Chain

Not long ago, the supply chain for retailing was quite simple. Manufacturers would ship their products to wholesalers who in turn would send the merchandise to department stores, grocery stores, and other retail outlets. Consumers, in turn, would make their purchases at the local mom-and-pop shop or nearby department store or in a store located in a mall if they lived in the suburbs. As retailing evolved, consumers could order products through a mail order catalog. And the introduction of a toll-free 800 number for ordering without having to leave one's home made shopping a relatively seamless experience—which was made famous by such well-known retailers as Sears and L.L.Bean.

The commercialization of the Internet has led to one of the greatest shifts in consumer spending in history. Instead of the traditional supply chain, e-commerce has created a more "layered" distribution of goods from the manufacturer to the customer. Now, manufacturers can send their goods not only via the long-standing supply chain but also to a regional distribution center, which in turn would send the merchandise to a "front distribution center (FDC)." The FDC has the option of sending directly to the retailer or to the customer. In addition, the wholesaler now has three options in the supply chain; the merchandise can be shipped to the regional distribution center, the front distribution center, or the retailer.[18]

E-commerce has caused a substantial transformation of consumer shopping habits and has created additional challenges for retailers, online platforms, and manufacturers. Consumers want quick, free shipping and free return shipping. At a minimum, consumers want merchandise delivered in two days and to be able to return an item hassle-free, which means receiving a return shipping label with packaging. This obviously poses both challenges and opportunities. E-commerce retailers have had to invest heavily in automation, artificial intelligence (AI), logistics, and other tools to get products out the door as rapidly as possible, and to be able to satisfy customers who were dissatisfied with their purchase.

Consumers, being tech savvy these days, comparison shop to get the best deal possible creating enormous price pressures for retailers. Unless productivity rises for online retailers, profit margins will tend to be squeezed as consumers scan to comparison shop on their smart phones in a brick-and-mortar store and see what the best deals are online. In fact, a strong case can be made that one of the reasons consumer price inflation has been kept at bay for the past 20 years, especially on the goods side, is the fierce competition for the consumers' dollars. Consumers have more information at their fingertips than they ever had before, and retailers therefore have to be superefficient to maintain sales in the most competitive retail environment in our history. Thus, the long-term secular trend in retail prices should be down for the reasons stated previously. The phrase "The consumer is king" is more appropriate today than at anytime since the first department store was opened in the 19th century.

Price deflation is the hallmark of a free market economy but has been interrupted by bouts of price inflation, which we have witnessed prior to the creation of the Federal Reserve in 1913 and since then. Inasmuch as consumer price inflation has been in a downward trend for four decades, will this trend continue or will another price inflation cycle unfold in the 2020s? If consumer prices will accelerate in the future, what does this portend for the retail supply chain?

During the boom phase of the business cycle, consumer prices in general tend to rise or even rise moderately and occasionally decline, as was the case during the Roaring Twenties. Each product and service therefore has an "inflation cycle" over the course of the economy's boom and bust. A price index does not capture the dynamics of individual sectors and companies within those sectors. If consumer demand were robust in some sectors, manufacturers and then retailers would be able to pass along higher costs to consumers. If consumers were price-sensitive, they would tend to balk at higher prices or seek out lower price alternatives. This poses a challenge for both manufacturers and retailers, namely, how much of their costs would they be able to pass on to consumers during the boom phase of the cycle? On the other hand, if prices in general are rising (e.g., the double-digit price inflation of the 1970s), consumers may be making pre-emptive purchases in order to avoid higher prices in the future. This is one of the defenses consumers have to protect themselves from rising prices during the boom. And when the recession begins with unemployment climbing and consumers become more anxious about keeping their jobs, even as price inflation is moderating, they will tend to reduce their purchases of discretionary items such as jewelry, clothing, new automobiles, and any other merchandise that could be postponed for an indefinite period of time during the downturn and possibly into the early months of the ensuing upswing in the economy.

What tactics and strategies could corporate managers and small business owners implement to deal with the challenges of the business cycle? One obvious tactic is to lock in prices of goods for upcoming seasonal merchandise in the expectation of higher wholesale prices. If retailers and wholesalers contract with manufacturers a set price months before production, then they could reap the benefits of higher price inflation in general as the new money that has been created "trickles down" to consumers in the later phase of the boom cycle. The downside to this tactic is that manufactures may want retailers and wholesalers to commit to a certain amount of production to lock in a price. That could be problematic if final demand does not materialize as much as businesses expect for the inventory that has been purchased in anticipation of higher prices and sales. Nevertheless, managers and small business owners could "do nothing" and pay higher prices as the merchandise moves along the supply chain and then observe consumer reactions to the price inflation. Creative marketing then would be needed to move the higher priced merchandise such as "Beat the price hikes. Buy now!" campaign or other inducements to keep real sales from declining. Thus, if retailers have extensive knowledge of their customers' needs and wants and price sensitivities, they should be able to navigate the challenges during the inflationary boom.

As the recession unfolds, retailers may find that consumers are even more price-sensitive as economic uncertainty pervades society. During the economic downturn, profit margins would be under pressure as sales may be flat or declining and costs may still be rising. Retailers then could be in a position to get price concessions from wholesalers and/or manufacturers in order to move merchandise to the consumer. For retailers, therefore, it would be prudent to have more than one or two wholesalers in their supply chain so they could survive the bust phase of the cycle and be in a position to thrive when the next upswing in the economy begins.

Conclusion

The business cycle, unfortunately, will be with us for the foreseeable future. As long as the Federal Reserve creates new money and manages (manipulates) short-term interest rates, the U.S. economy will experience periodic booms and busts. That's the bad news. The good news is that inventors, innovators, and entrepreneurs will continue to provide consumers with new and better products. That has been the history of business since the beginning of the republic. Unfortunately, the pandemic of 2020, which may have had the greatest transformative impact on the structure of American businesses and the supply chain, has already caused winners and losers to emerge (as of this writing at the end of 2020) in the so-called new normal.

That pandemic has caused most, if not all, businesses to rethink the supply chain they depended upon before COVID-19 hit America's shores. Businesses that have depended upon some of their inputs from overseas may be realizing that globalization—the international division of labor and specialization—may be unreliable as geopolitics, tariffs, and health concerns may make them seek domestic supply chain partners to replace foreign sources of raw materials, intermediate goods, and consumer merchandise. Nevertheless, the long-term decline in U.S. manufacturing may have ended with the pandemic, according to economics professor Douglas A. Irwin. Writing in the *Wall Street Journal*, Irwin observes, "there is a natural tendency to turn inward and reduce dependence on others. People begin to value security more than efficiency."[19] In the same *Wall Street Journal* issue, Scott Davis, chairman and CEO of Melius Research, notes that manufacturing is making a comeback because of the pandemic. He points out that the winners in 2020 include hardware stores and HVAC suppliers as Americans have been improving their homes with the resources they otherwise would have been spending on restaurants, traveling, and other purchases.[20] Davis' optimism is based upon the localization of the supply chain and the innovative factors—data analytics, cloud computing, and AI—which will make American manufacturing more competitive in the global economy. He also reports that investments in these areas have provided widespread benefits such as "higher safety levels, higher employees' morale, lower turnover among staff, higher quality control, faster new-product cycles, and lower environmental impacts." In other words, U.S. manufacturing may be entering a new Golden age.

On the retail front, well-known clothing brands have decided to begin selling their upscale products at Target, Walmart, and Tractor Supply Company. The strategy has paid off for such brands as Levi Strauss, Steve Madden, and others who realized that their lower-priced brands would not be cannibalized and the foot traffic at the big-box stores would bring in consumers to purchase their full-price items.[21]

Entrepreneurs are adapting to the new normal as the fallout from the pandemic of 2020 unfolds. Unfortunately, the restaurant industry has taken a huge hit throughout the country as thousands of restaurants have already closed and thousands more are on the brink of closing their doors as 2021 begins.

To survive and thrive in the new normal of a postpandemic world with another economic downturn inevitable, corporate managers and small business owners will be put to the test to recognize the business cycle turning point and take appropriate actions to increase profitability, gain market share, or form strategic alliances.

The next chapter will focus on how businesses can improve their workforces during the economy's boom and bust.

CHAPTER 6

Strengthening the Workforce

A business is like a cake or any other item prepared in a kitchen—it needs a recipe with several key ingredients to "come out just right." The master chef is the entrepreneur who is the driving force pursing value for consumers. The two essential factors that an entrepreneur "orchestrates" for a company to survive—and thrive—are capital investment and a productive workforce. Additional key ingredients include a reliable supply chain and vital external factors such as reasonable regulations, and tax and trade policies that do not encumber business operations.[1] And of course an economy needs a financial system that makes it possible for entrepreneurs to raise funds for both long- and short-term needs. A major corollary to a sound financial system is to have a medium exchange (money) that is not devalued and an interest rate environment where a key price signal does not fluctuate at the whims of a central authority. In short, the best possible business outcomes occur in a free market with sound money.

Although the United States does not have a pure free market economy, entrepreneurs have been able to create, innovate, and produce goods and services for the American people despite the various government interventions of the past 200 plus years since the founding of the republic. In other words, the unsung heroes of the American experience are entrepreneurs, who have continued to improve living standards for the public through depressions, banking panics, double-digit inflation, political assignations, declared and undeclared wars, and burdensome regulations. In this chapter, we will focus on one of the key ingredients of a successful business—the tens of millions of workers throughout the structure of production who are impacted during the business cycle—and most of the 2020 pandemic.

The U.S. economy has grown for more than 80 years, and the number of working Americans has increased from 29.9 million in January 1939 to 152.5 million in February 2020, just before the lockdowns began as the pandemic unfolded (see Figure 6.1), which caused a sharp drop in the number of employed. The subsequent snapback occurred as more states

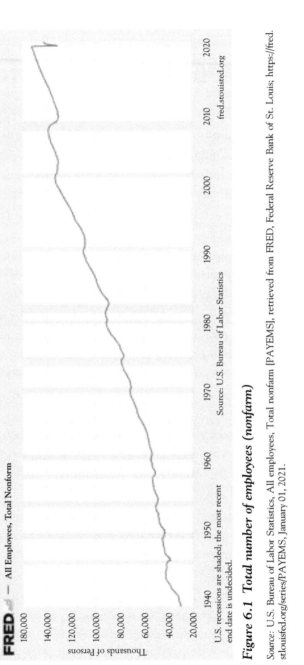

Figure 6.1 Total number of employees (nonfarm)

Source: U.S. Bureau of Labor Statistics, All employees, Total nonfarm [PAYEMS], retrieved from FRED, Federal Reserve Bank of St. Louis; https://fred.stlouisfed.org/series/PAYEMS, January 01, 2021.

opened up their economies. As 2020 ended, the number of employees is still below the all-time high reached earlier in the year.

The graph reveals the long-term secular trend in U.S. employment and the cyclical fluctuations that take place during the boom-bust cycle (see Figure 6.2). When the total employment data is disaggregated, manufacturing employment skyrocketed during World War II and reached a secular peak in July 1979 at 19.5 million. Then, manufacturing employment began a steady decline until bottoming out in February 2010 at 11.5 million. The precipitous fall in manufacturing employment during the pandemic was followed by a sharp rebound but still below the prepandemic peak at the end of 2020. The jury is still out as to whether manufacturing employment will increase in this decade because of the shaky supply chain during the pandemic. If U.S. manufacturing employment has a resurgence, manufacturers will have concluded they want to have a more secure supply chain by shifting production from overseas.

Construction employment—one of the most sensitive sectors of the economy—reached a post–Great Depression trough during World War II (September 1944) at slightly more than 1 million and reached a peak in

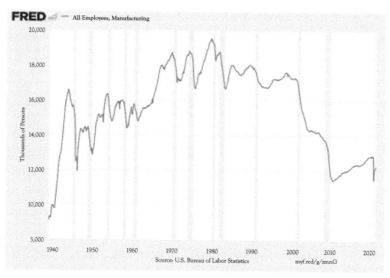

Figure 6.2 Number of manufacturing employees

Source: U.S. Bureau of Labor Statistics, All employees, manufacturing [MANEMP], retrieved from FRED, Federal Reserve Bank of St. Louis; https://fred.stlouisfed.org/series/MANEMP, January 02, 2021.

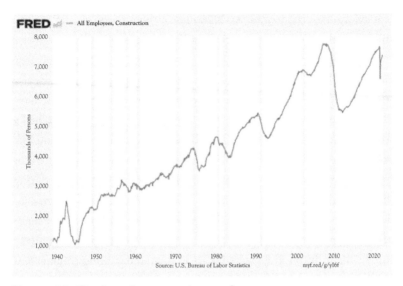

Figure 6.3 Number of construction employees

Source: U.S. Bureau of Labor Statistics, All employees, construction [USCONS], retrieved from FRED, Federal Reserve Bank of St. Louis; https://fred.stlouisfed.org/series/USCONS, January 2, 2021.

August 2006 at 7.7 million before the housing bubble burst (see Figure 6.3). In contrast, one of the emerging employment trends in the United States has been in professional and technical services. Based on the trends of the past three decades, the future is bright for college graduates in computer science, AI, data analytics, and other high-tech fields (see Figure 6.4).[2]

Furloughs, Layoffs, and the Business Cycle

During the boom phase of the business cycle, employment is robust and labor shortages may appear in certain sectors of the economy, boosting wages and salaries in the most sensitive industries such as mining, construction, and transportation. Employers may also find it difficult to attract workers in retailing, food services, and other businesses without raising wages. Employees would be attracted to the "higher order" businesses if they have the skills or would be willing to be trained for employment in industries where wages and salaries are rising the fastest. Thus, easy money policies set into motion a relative rearrangement of employment throughout the structure of production with enormous implications for when the bust phase of the economy unfolds.[3]

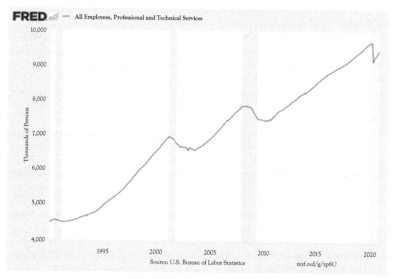

Figure 6.4 Number of professional and technical services employees

Source: U.S. Bureau of Labor Statistics, All employees, professional and technical services [CES6054000001], retrieved from FRED, Federal Reserve Bank of St. Louis; https://fred.stlouisfed. org/series/CES6054000001, January 02, 2021.

When an economic downturn begins, an employer has three options in the face of declining sales—furloughs, layoffs, or a reduction in force (RIF).[4] If employers are confident that their sales will pick up in the not too distant future, they may furlough employees with the prospect of bringing them back relatively soon and therefore not lose skilled employees. Employees, on the other hand, have to be confident that the furlough would be short term and they would regain their positions relatively quickly once the economy is in another up cycle. This may be a great leap of faith on their part, but if employees are content receiving unemployment benefits until they are recalled, this could be a win-win for both employer and employee. Employees would not have to incur the additional expenses in hiring and training new employees when the upswing begins, and employees would be able to return to positions in the company that they have performed well, built up seniority, have opportunities for advancement, and other benefits.

Another option for employers is to lay off workers with the prospect of bringing them back, because the economic slowdown has contracted sales and employers are confident they can rehire the laid-off employees after the business turns around. Although a layoff seems similar to a furlough, the latter may be for a few weeks or a couple of months, while a layoff is usually indefinite. When an employer realizes business will not pick up as soon as it thought, a layoff may become permanent. That's when an employer decides to reduce the businesses head count, with a reduction in force.

One tactic employers can utilize to weather an economic storm is to cut salaries of upper management first and then frontline workers to avoid furloughing or laying off employees. This action could be a morale booster and signal to employees that "We are all in this together."[5]

As the pandemic hit, the CEO of MasterCard, Ajay Banga, made a commitment to the company's 19,000 employees: there would be no layoffs during the crisis. He explained his decision in a *New York Times* interview at the end of 2020.

> It was the right thing to do. One thing we didn't need to do at a time like this was to add more fuel to the fire by making our employees insecure, by making them worry about their jobs, as compared to worry about their health and their family. It was a very easy decision.

So he told our people,

> Focus on your health, on your family, then focus on your clients and your work stop worrying about your job.[6]

Other employees around America have not been so fortunate as the *New York Times* reported in October 2020.[7] The dozen individuals profiled in all regions of the country from all demographics and primarily earning average salaries provided a microcosm of the damage caused by the lockdowns in response to the pandemic. Some of the individuals persisted in their job hunt and eventually found a new job.

There is no one-size-fits-all tactic for employers to use when a downturn occurs because of a recession or a pandemic. The prudent approach would be for managers and business owners to forecast as best as they can what the next 6, 12, and 18 months would look like for their companies.

Once they are confident in their economic forecasts, they can then determine which tactic(s) they should implement to survive the downturn and subsequently thrive in the next cyclical expansion. In fact, managers and small business owners should plan before the downturn arrives to avoid making decisions under pressure.

Intrapreneurship: Tapping the Workforce

An entrepreneur is like a chef mixing the essential ingredients of business to dish out a new product or service. Most Americans can identify past entrepreneurs—Ford, Edison, Carnegie, Rockefeller, among others—and the current generation of movers and shakers such as Gates, Bezos, Zuckerberg, the late Steve Jobs, and others who have had an enormous impact on American business, creating millions of jobs in high-tech and other industries. But entrepreneurship is only part of the American business success story.

Although the term *intrapreneurship* was coined more than four decades ago, and is defined as "a person within an existing organization that takes direct responsibility for turning an idea into a profitable finished product via assertive risk-taking and innovation,"[8] the single most important factor that will propel the future of American business could be tapping the ingenuity of a firm's employees.[9]

And in a 1985 *Newsweek* article, Steve Jobs described the team that created the Macintosh as an example of Intrapreneurship where, "a group of people [are] going, in essence, back to the garage, but in a large company."[10] Large companies, therefore, have all the ingredients for innovative employees to create the next big thing for the firm to increase sales and profitability and for the general public to reap the benefits of new products and services. A win-win-win for businesses, entrepreneurial employees, and customers.

Corporations that have encouraged Intrapreneurship have devoted funds for dedicated research and development departments, internal incubators, and special events.[11] According to a senior product manager at Amazon, Rovina Broomfield, who is in charge of an incubator at the firm, "Amazon's culture encourages innovation in many ways."[12]

Other intrapreneurs have used their skills and knowledge at a start-up or at a relatively new company to mitigate some of the risk entrepreneurs have to deal with by having a steady income and not having to deal with all of the financial, management, and marketing issues of a company they created.[13] Recent successful Intrapreneurship projects have occurred in such diverse companies as Sony, Facebook, Intel, Lockheed Martin, and DreamWorks.[14]

Corporate managers who want to begin an Intrapreneurship initiative in their companies should review the insights compiled by Deloitte Digital.[15] This 2015 white paper contains numerous suggestions to accelerate innovation in a company, especially insight five, which requires management to take a whole new approach to administering their organizations. According to insight two, "Intrapreneurship pays off many times over in terms of company growth, culture, and talent."[16] From a historical perspective, the rapid changes in American business cannot be overstated, 88 percent of the companies in the S&P 500 in 1955 were no longer in existence by 2015 either because of a merger or acquisition, or they fell by the wayside. Business sustainability is not a given and thus in our fast changing world, it would behoove managers to tap their internal talent to remain a viable standalone enterprise. In other words, history is not on the side of managers who are content with the status quo but on the side of managers who realize that Intrapreneurship is a key component of a company's overall strategy.

Building an Effective Workforce

An effective workforce, goes without saying, is crucial for a business' success. If employees are not "tap dancing to work," productivity will be problematic, and the firm's sales and customer satisfaction may be damaged, thus negatively impacting the bottom line.[17] However, during the boom phase of the business cycle, where there is general prosperity across virtually all business sectors—rising wages, increasing sales, and higher profits—a firm's internal weaknesses may not be apparent to managers as they may overlook issues that may become threats as long as the bottom line is increasing. Nevertheless, for some firms the boom phase of the cycle poses an interesting challenge, namely finding enough workers for key positions throughout the organization. Thus, worker productivity may not be at optimal levels during the boom. And when the inevitable downturn unfolds, that's when worker anxiety becomes evident, productivity may take a dive, and absenteeism could become a problem.

What are the best practices for both corporate managers and small-business owners to implement to build an effective workforce during both phases of the business cycle?

To build an effective workforce, companies need to refine their workforce planning and be able to project their need for human capital. Metrics that predict the demand for products moving forward will allow companies to hire their workforce in advance. This will allow demand to be met as well as quality service for customers. Businesses will be better prepared to align their capital resources with their demand's levels, and this includes their human capital. If they are understaffed when demand increases, they will have problems repeating that revenue, and they will have missed out of growing the business as well as the profits that could have been achieved.

Small business managers have numerous ways to motivate their employees such as rewarding problem solvers, soliciting feedback, delegating team tasks, growing from mistakes, and helping with career paths.[18] Building a coherent team is crucial in a small business inasmuch as a disgruntled employee could have a harmful impact on morale and therefore productivity, which would have negative effect on profits. In short, managers "must anticipate and react to changes, well at the same time maintaining a clear and concise employee management plan and vision."[19]

On the other side of the business spectrum, corporations such as Amazon, AT&T, Chipotle, McDonald's, and Walmart have realized that helping entry-level and mid-level employees with education assistance is an important factor for increasing their bottom lines and building an effective workforce.[20]

Con-way Freight is one company that has learned to effectively manage its workforce. After the 2009 recession, Con-way laid off 2,300 employees but then lowered its pricing to gain market share. This quickly led to unforeseen demand for its trucking services, and it had to rapidly hire unexpectedly. This caused service quality to deteriorate, employee engagement to decline, and training costs to rise. But Con-way Freight learned from this, and it started to plan its hiring off of city forecasts in order to meet the time that hiring takes, which is one to three months in the trucking industry. Also, in order to combat the driver shortage, the company has developed a program where they allow its part-time dock-workers to attend driving schools. This gives the company the opportunity to hire individuals that align with its culture and company values. It is a symbiotic relationship that both parties have a stake in since Conway pays for their truck schooling. This company is an example of how optimized relationships and training programs will allow the company to meet its demand needs with an efficient workforce.

As the pandemic of 2020 took its toll on American businesses—large and small—managers were faced with an enormous challenge "out of left field"—how to maintain morale in an unprecedented time in which there was no playbook to get remedies. Nevertheless, in a recent *Wall Street Journal* article, Rachel Feintzeig provided some helpful hints for managers such as organizing Zoom meetings with a specific purpose, analyzing team projects quickly to provide feedback to members, challenging workers to address an overriding issue, keeping track of employee progress, and reminding workers that hopefully the "pandemic economy" will not last forever.[21]

As the U.S. economy continues to evolve, an effective workforce in the coming age of AI is being able to respond to data trends and predict the hiring cycles. If a company realizes there is a hiring shortage at the time it is happening, then it is already too late. AI will allow the blending of many different hiring goals to build an effective workforce. AI will be able to give us way more in-depth details of trends and employee skillsets. The ability to identify employee-behavior analysis will give organizations tools to refine their workforce to the tasks they are most successful at. It will optimize efficiency in the workplace, and organizations will be having access to more data than ever before. The challenge will be to optimize it in the most efficient way to increase the company's value. Humans will be able to spend more time reasoning, coordinating, and then making decisions instead of having to process the information that is told by the data.[22]

CHAPTER 7

Expansions, Mergers, and Other Opportunities

The boom phase of the business cycle is fueled by "cheap money"—that is, the Federal Reserve injecting new money into the banking system. This increase in liquidity causes short-term interest rates to fall to levels below what the free market would have determined by the interplay of supply and demand of savers and borrowers. The Fed's actions set into motion an unsustainable period of economic activity throughout the structure of production and "irrational exuberance" in the financial markets, especially the stock market. The inevitable bust arrives when the Federal Reserve raises interest rates by withdrawing liquidity from the financial system to dampen the overheated economy. In short, the Federal Reserve causes the systematic ups and downs of the economy in its attempt to "smooth out" the business cycle (which it causes), keep employment robust, and maintain a target annual price inflation rate of 2 percent.

As we have shown in previous chapters, the Federal Reserve's track record leaves much to be desired. Both the dot-com and the housing bubbles confirm the consequences of the Federal Reserve's easy money policies. And the current boom that began in 2009 which was interrupted by the coronavirus pandemic in 2020 will eventually end when the Federal Reserve "tightens" credit conditions to deal with the overheated economy.

Other consequences of the Federal Reserve's easy money policies can also be identified during a business cycle. During the boom phase, corporate managers and small business owners tend to be reasonably—and at times wildly—optimistic about future business conditions. Corporate CEOs in virtually all sectors of the economy view the economic expansion as an opportunity to grow their businesses beyond what the free market would have signaled them to do and/or "hunt" for takeover candidates. Small business owners, on the other hand, see the upswing in economic activity as an opportunity to enlarge their current location, or expand their businesses by opening up new locations or creating a franchise business model. The challenge, therefore, for all business decision makers is to determine what actions to take during the boom phase of the cycle that are sustainable and not based on the euphoria caused by the Fed's easy money policies. In this chapter, we will examine three actions business decision makers can undertake as the business cycle unfolds—developing economies of scale, expansion opportunities, and mergers.

Economists, management consultants, and other experts have been analyzing the benefits of economies of scale for generations. One insight that has been gleaned from the study of this phenomenon is the concept of agglomeration. The creation of "clusters" such as Silicon Valley, which emerged from the intellectual expertise at Stanford University, allowed economies of scale to develop by bringing together skilled workers, complementary firms, and venture capitalists to a unique location that has been "difficult to duplicate."[1] The automobile industry was and is a classic example of agglomeration in Detroit for decades, as General Motors, Ford, and Chrysler made the Motor City one of the successful urban centers during the heyday of American dominance in the motor vehicle sector. The clustering of an industry also is an example of how companies that are geographically close could share knowledge through licensing and other arrangements.

Nevertheless, as the United States has been evolving for the past 60 years to more of a service-oriented, high-tech, and digital-age economy, economies of scale have become less important as a strategy and tactic. Instead, entrepreneurs would be better served if they kept their eye on the ball and focused on the economics of value.[2]

The economics of value highlights the alternative approaches to economies of scale. The traditional economies of scale can be summed up as "bigger is better" to the extent that entrepreneurs can increase production, lower costs, and increase profitability. The focus of economies of scale is "product centric," while the economics of value concentrates on consumer satisfaction "so that they can experience the maximum (subjective) value."

Small businesses with a well-defined niche in the marketplace can implement the economics of value strategy seamlessly by focusing their energies on customer service, product exclusivity, and brand differentiation. With e-commerce exploding in the number and amount of transactions in the past 10 years, the retailers that have thrived met consumers' needs—an easy online purchase experience, free shipping, and free returns and exchanges. The economics of value can thus be implemented by businesses of all sizes.

According to the economics of value, because "scale can be rented"— by using Amazon Marketplace or cloud computing—entrepreneurs do not need to "scale up" and incur more uncertainty.[3] However, if (sustainable) business conditions warrant scaling up, then the decision to maintain the economics of value should be paramount to reap the rewards of satisfying customers' needs. In other words, by maintaining a high-value consumer experience, repeat business is the entrepreneur's best outcome, which is in many ways no different than an annuity, a steady cash flow to the small business owner, or the corporation.

Even if entrepreneurs are "doing everything right' as far as consumer satisfaction and providing value are concerned, what happens to sales and profitability when the inevitable downturn unfolds and consumers retrench? This begs the question: what sector is the business in? The most economic-sensitive, like housing, autos, discretionary goods and services such as jewelry, travel, and so forth? Or, is the business in the nondiscretionary sector that performs relatively well during a recession—businesses that deal in consumer staples, utilities, health care, and the like? The answer to these questions would result in taking actions during the early stages of the boom to take advantage of the robust economy and then preparing for the downturn. The skill of business decision makers to navigate the ebbs and flows of changing conditions would be reflected in the company's bottom line. As the COVID-19 pandemic caught virtually all businesses totally off guard (who could have planned for such a phenomenon and the subsequent lockdowns and business contraction?), the unfortunate reality is that thousands of businesses have permanently closed for no fault of their own and their owners and employees must either start all over or go to work for someone else.

Expansion Opportunities

Once a business experiences success, the natural tendency is to expand at the current location or build a new plant closer to consumers or open another retail store in the same city, county, or state. Seldom, however, would a retail store open a second location in another state.

The primary goal of expanding a business would be to attract new customers. One example would be a comic book storeowner expanding the square footage of the premises and invite local artists to display their original works.[4] The increase in foot traffic could potentially bring in new comic book customers and provide an income stream for the storeowner, whether it is renting the space out or taking a percentage of the artists' sales.

Another expansion opportunity would be to develop an additional revenue stream in the same location. For example, a bakery could expand its operations by creating a small restaurant to serve breakfast and lunch.[5] With the 2020 pandemic in the backdrop, takeout meals or a small sitting area for customers would not require a major investment to generate revenue and increase the bakery's bottom line. Even with more people working remotely, local bakeries with a dining component would provide individuals an opportunity to take a break and visit their local businesses for a snack or take out meal.

The food business is the least sensitive sector during the business cycle and undoubtedly provides "comfort and joy" to remote worker while also giving them the opportunity to stretch their legs during the day. So small food businesses, depending upon the zoning codes and other local regulations, could partner with a baker or chef. A local boutique, jewelry store, or high tech business could benefit by having an additional income stream from a food or any other well-suited business. The risk for the small business owner would be relatively minimal, especially if the partner picks up the expansion costs, and the return on investment could be relatively high.

Other methods to expand sales include creating a customer loyalty program, building an e-mail list, forming strategic partnerships, making licensing deals, franchising the business, expanding internationally, diversifying the product line, or offering new services. Those are among some of the strategies that could be utilized to grow a business by making relatively minor capital expenditures.[6]

Before any of these strategies are undertaken, a committee could be formed at the corporate level to investigate each one of these approaches to find out which ones will provide the greatest bang for the buck. For small business, a consultant could be hired or the owner and partners (if there are any) could begin to do the research if they are so inclined. No matter what the size of a business is, having the most reliable information is imperative to make an informed decision regarding expansion opportunities. For small business, a misstep could be fatal and costly when trying to expand business. For incorporated businesses expansions are not a dunk shot. Even mega corporations can stumble—like Coca-Cola's misstep with the introduction of Coke light in 2013; the company had to drop it from its product portfolio a few years later.[7]

One of the tempting expansion opportunities is to go international by opening up an overseas manufacturing operation and/or retail locations. The standard benefits are increased sales and profitability as well as numerous other advantages—such as new market penetration, accessing local talent, beating your competition, and establishing regional centers to provide established international customers with numerous services.[8] Before going it alone in Europe, South America, Africa, or Asia, a business should investigate establishing an alliance—partnership with a successful overseas corporation, a U.S. multinational or a local business.

Although the desire to expand internationally may be a strategic goal, it comes with various amounts of risk, especially if the company wants to go it alone. The cost of establishing an overseas presence and the costs of possibly having to terminate operations could be very costly especially for small and medium-size businesses. The risks and costs of complying with local and national regulations may be daunting. Understanding the cultural and business practices overseas to have a successful presence maybe a hurdle too high to overcome. Thus, before stepping into the international pond, so to speak, managers and small business owners would need to obtain substantial data and information about how to have a successful outcome. Tapping the expertise of an international business consultant would probably be one of the first steps a business owner would do before deciding to expand overseas. In other words, it would be better to know not to enter an overseas market than to enter a market and incur expenses and show no return on investment.

Nevertheless, an expansion strategy allows a company to diversify its "portfolio" that could have different sensitivities to business cycles. Thus, a firm with four or five subsidiaries could have a company or companies that are highly profitable during the boom but whose profits decline or may turn into losses during the bust. It is during the downturn in the economy that the firm could be in financial distress and not recover. Therefore, adding a relatively noncyclical company or company to a firm's portfolio would "smooth out" its profitability over the course of the business cycle.

Mergers and Other Opportunities

The so-called urge to merge has not been dampened despite the fact that up to 90 percent of mergers do not work out well.[9] Call it empire building, ego gratification, or just plain old speculation with shareholders' money, corporate managers are prone to paying exorbitant prices for so-called trophy businesses. Doug French summarizes the risks associated with corporate mergers.[10] French distills the works of several accountants, business consultants, and economists who highlight the traps involved in corporate mergers.

One of the key variables in the evaluation process of an acquired company is the discount rate, which is applied to future earnings to determine its present value and the future terminal value of the enterprise. A low interest rate will therefore increase the net present value of the potential acquired firm and justify a relatively high price. However, if the interest rate is "depressed" because the Federal Reserve has injected liquidity into the financial system, corporate managers in essence will be fooled by the mispriced cost of capital and thus overbid for the acquired company. Thus, during the boom phase of the cycle, especially when the Federal Reserve is keeping interest rates down to stimulate employment and production, mergers and acquisitions (M&A) tend to accelerate because the cost of capital makes it attractive for corporate managers to go on an acquisition spree.[11]

Kison Patel has compiled a list of the eight biggest M&A failures of all-time, and concluded,[12]

It's easy to sell the idea of a retail bank buying a mortgage provider, a traditional toy maker merging with a technology platform or a software maker buying a handset maker to shareholders. But a narrative isn't enough. You can overpay for a company, which may even be a good, fit (AOL/Time Warner), misunderstand the dynamics of a market (Google and Nokia) or simply not perform enough due diligence (Bank of America and Countrywide). Avoiding M&A failures means paying more attention to details like these and less to the grand narrative behind the deal.

Some recent mergers include the following:

America Online and Time Warner (2001):	U.S.$65 billion
Daimler-Benz and Chrysler (1998):	U.S.$36 billion
Google and Motorola (2012):	U.S.$12.5 billion
Microsoft and Nokia (2013):	U.S.$7 billion
KMart and Sears (2005):	U.S.$11 billion
eBay and Skype (2005):	U.S.$2.6 billion
Bank of America and Countrywide (2008):	U.S.$2 billion
Mattel and The Learning Company (1998):	U.S.$3.8 billion

Virtually all these mergers took place during the boom phase of the business cycle. America Online's (AOL) acquisition of Time Warner occurred when the economy was in recession and AOL management undoubtedly thought there would be enormous synergies between it and entertainment giant Time Warner. And Bank of America acquired Countrywide during the Great Recession of 2008, when the Federal Reserve and U.S. Treasury induced the largest banks in the country to acquire financial institutions that were in terrible shape when the housing bubble burst.

Fast forward to 2016 when AT&T announced it would merge with Time Warner. After a trial in which the Justice Department objected to the merger, the U.S. District Court in Washington, DC, decided the merger could go ahead and AT&T's $85 billion takeover was finalized. Time will tell if this time Time Warner has found a long-term home in the telecommunications giant's portfolio.

Some mergers that have so far proved sustainable include Unilever's purchase of Ben & Jerry's in 2000. Under the terms of the agreement, the Vermont-based ice cream maker retains its own board of directors and continues its social mission.[13] Before Facebook went public in 2012, Mark Zuckerberg decided to make a strategic investment and purchased

Instagram for $1 billion, even though the photo sharing service had no revenue.[14] Several years later (2017), Amazon purchased Whole Foods for $13.7 billion, giving the giant e-commerce retailer huge presence in the brick-and-mortar retail sector.[15] A year later, privately held Belkin was purchased for $866 million by unit of Foxconn Technology Group, the Taiwanese-based assembler of Apple's iPhones.[16] Chet Pipkin founded Belkin nearly four decades ago in his parents' house and "cashed out" to a major overseas company, but still runs the company and thrives in solving problems, especially during the Covid epidemic.

One entrepreneur, Brynn Putnam, whose company, Mirror, thrived during the pandemic sold the at-home fitness product to Lululemon Athletica Inc., for $500 million.[17] Although she sold the company, she still runs the business and reports to the CEO, Calvin McDonald, of Lululemon. With sales rising robustly as the pandemic forced more individuals to work at home and exercise there as well, Putnam felt it would be wise to let Mirror be purchased by a successful clothing retailer, which would allow her "baby," her creation, to thrive in the future.[18]

In the aforementioned examples, the founders of these companies decided to reap the benefits of their entrepreneurial efforts and be taken over by deep pocket companies who could take their businesses to the next level of success. Creating a company, finding a niche in the marketplace, and applying proven management, marketing, and financial expertise are the ingredients to provide value for consumers. The only merger that was based on speculation and strategic vision was the Facebook takeover of Instagram. Nevertheless, starting from scratch, these entrepreneurs became fabulously wealthy confirming that small businesses can survive and thrive over the course of several cycles (Belkin, Whole Foods, and Ben & Jerry's), while others (Instagram and Mirror) was scooped up by companies that saw the potential strategic benefits of the takeovers.

From a tactical perspective, both small business owners and corporate managers can, more often than not, take advantage of depressed asset prices during an economic downturn to purchase a rival or a business that would fit in a corporation's portfolio. Purchasing assets at well below replacement or book value could be one of the most optimal methods to grow a business with lower risk. As Warren Buffett once famously said during the 1973–1974 bear market, he felt like he was a kid in a candy store when the stock prices of great companies were selling for 40 percent, 50 percent, or more below their previous highs. Buffett outlined his approach to buying stocks in a *New York Times* op-ed (October 16, 2008) when he reiterated his tactic for buying stocks: "A simple rule dictates my buying: Be fearful when others are greedy, and be greedy when others are fearful."[19] Although the stock market didn't hit bottom until March 2009, Buffett's insights about the ebbs and flows of the financial markets have served Berkshire Hathaway's shareholders well for the more than 55 years he has been the CEO. Buffett's approach can also be applied to purchasing privately held companies at favorable prices when economic conditions are depressed. In a downturn, small business owners may decide the depressed economic conditions are too much to deal with and decide to sell to get out from under the burden of falling sales and declining profitability or losses.

The bottom line is that corporate managers and small business owners need to have the wherewithal—cash reserves and/or access to capital—during a downturn to make strategic purchases. Inasmuch as market fluctuations are marked by fear and greed of investors and business owners, there will always be opportunities to purchase quality companies at attractive prices when the opportunities arise.

CHAPTER 8

Small Business

Small business epitomizes the American dream. From tinkering in the basement or garage to organizing a new business at the dining room table or college dorm room, entrepreneurs have been creating their versions of the American dream since the beginning of the republic. Some of the most notable start-up businesses that began as a vision of one or more individuals and became giants include Apple, Microsoft, Dell, Amazon, Facebook, Netflix, and countless others that have become behemoths across numerous sectors of the U.S. economy. Nevertheless, small business failures, which may be overstated, are caused by many factors.[1] Small business owners can improve their chances of success if they understand the vulnerabilities they may encounter and have the "entrepreneurial mindset" before they embark on their pursuit of the American dream.

A successful small business owner typically should have some knowledge of accounting, finance, marketing, and other business skills to manage effectively. Another indispensable tool or scale that small-business owners must master is "empathy."[2] Empathy is nothing less than understanding what motivates the consumer, how your product or service would alleviate his/her "uneasiness" and, in the final analysis, would provide better value than your competitors.[3]

The goal, therefore, of a small business owner is not to be "self-employed" but to be a value creator.[4] "The role of the entrepreneurs is to figure out how to provide value to consumers and how much to charge for it."[5] The manager's role, on the other hand, is to keep an eye on the company's costs in order to generate profits. A small business owner's marching orders are fairly straightforward: know your customers' needs and goals, determine the value you can provide, and the price you can charge for your good or service, and put together a "recipe"—the business structure model—that would generate a profit. Over time, a small business could grow into a medium or large enterprise as we've seen in the evolution of the Amazons, Facebooks, and Apples of the business world.

A successful small business not only provides value to consumers but also helps improve the lives of workers.[6] Competition among small businesses for workers, as well as competing with big-box stores and other large enterprises for talented employees, means one thing, workers are in the driver's seat regarding salary and benefits. In fact, a case can be made that workers may be in a better bargaining position with small businesses, which may have to offer higher wages/salaries to attract talented employees. Moreover, minority and women-owned small businesses (with employees) totaled more than two million in 2017, according to the Census Bureau, the last year data were available.[7] In fact, in recent years, growth of small businesses was higher in minority communities than nonminority populations.[8] Owning the small business, therefore, has been, is, and will continue to be the best wealth generator for Americans—especially members of minority communities.

Vulnerabilities

Positive cash flow is to small business what air is to human beings—without it you die. New small business needs to be adequately capitalized in order to pay all its expenses and maintain its focus on creating value for customers. Once the business is up and running, the challenges are managing receivables, managing payments, especially payroll, and obtaining capital when necessary as the business grows.[9] Unless a small business owner has the accounting and finance skills to run a business, he/she should hire a financial consultant/accountant to navigate the cash flow challenges during the business' initial years. As the business grows and positive cash flow is steady, financial and accounting expertise becomes even more necessary.

Small businesses probably face the most competitive environment in our history. Businesses have to compete locally and regionally as well as nationally because of e-commerce. At the height of the holiday shopping season, customers use the Internet to compare prices to obtain the lowest price for products they are seeking. The small business, therefore, needs to differentiate its goods or services to meet the needs of customers by focusing on value. In addition, large brick-and-mortar stores carry many different products so customers can purchase everything they need in one store without having to travel to different ones. This is one of the greatest challenges facing small businesses; they cannot compete on price with Walmart or Amazon.

Another risk facing small businesses in an age of e-commerce is cyber security. Small businesses probably will not have their own IT cyber security team on site to protect their data. Without the proper precautions, they would be susceptible to ransomware attacks and hacking of their databases. A disruption in their IT systems could not only result in lost business but also open them up to lawsuits. A small business, therefore, could hire local talent either from a high school or a local college for a reasonable amount to help set up the appropriate defenses against an IT attack.

Other risks facing small businesses include interruptions from a storm, fire, or pandemic and supply chain interruptions, which would cause, for example, a manufacturing company to shut down its operations temporarily or for an extended period of time. In addition, small business owners could have a legal adviser and sufficient commercial general liability coverage to deal with wrongful employment practices, workers compensation claims, and environmental and pollution liability losses.[10] An additional vulnerability of small businesses is the loss of a key employee, which could be ameliorated by purchasing key person insurance. Lastly, insurance coverage for the loss of property, equipment, and electronic data is a must in an era where e-commerce is growing markedly, especially for small businesses.

Besides all the challenges a small business owner faces during so-called normal times, the fact that we live in a business cycle economy poses additional risks. One obvious challenge for small business owner is to attract competent employees during the boom phase of the cycle when all companies are scrambling to hire additional workers. The competition for workers will tend to raise salaries, which will put a squeeze on small business profitability. A small business owner should be able to maintain his staff as long as the employees perceive moving to another company may not be in their best interests even at a higher salary. The small business entrepreneur would have to put his "managerial" hat on to keep his employees in the fold so to speak to avoid incurring greater recruiting and training costs.

When the inevitable downturn occurs, small business owners will face a different challenge, namely, how to maintain profitability, retain the necessary staff to ride out the economic storm, and then prepare for the eventual upturn in the economy.

For fledgling small business owners, one of the best places to begin obtaining the tools necessary to travel successfully on the road of entrepreneurship would be HunterHastings.com and Economics for Business (https://mises.org/library/economics-business). These free tools are invaluable for any individual who is going to take the leap into becoming an entrepreneur. These two websites provide both a theoretical framework and practical advice for entrepreneurs. Embracing the insights of Hunter Hastings, other economists, and successful entrepreneurs would provide not only information that would help them launch their business but also provide experienced entrepreneurs with the set of tools to enhance their current operations.

Fluctuations, Bailing Out, Sticking It Out, Cashing Out

Small businesses are especially vulnerable to economic downturns, especially manufacturing companies.[11] Nevertheless, there are several sensible tactics a small business can use to ride out the financial storm. To recession-proof your business, Susan Ward recommends: protect your cash flow, review inventory management, focus on core competencies, win the competitor's customers, make the most of current customers, increase rather than decrease marketing, and monitor your credit scores.[12] Although there are no guarantees that a small business will survive by doing everything "right" during a recession, the probability that the company would avoid bankruptcy or liquidation would increase markedly.

Several examples of small business owners who were impacted by the great recession of 2008, but retooled/reorganized and survived include Rhys Williamson, whose fiberglass boat business revenues declined from $3m to $150k/year; he then pivoted, specializing in repair work. Robert Radcliff saw his consulting business revenue decline from $1.8m to $550k/year; he laid off his staff to stay afloat. Dida Clifton's bookkeeping business was cut in half; she stayed in business by entering into strategic partnerships. David Stringer's auto accessories business declined by 37 percent; to stay afloat he diversified his client pool.[13] There are undoubt-edly hundreds if not thousands of small business owners who had to rethink their business plans in order to survive and thrive after the Great Recession. It behooves small business owners to have contingency plans in place, as the current upswing in the business cycle is an opportune time for entrepreneurs to prepare for the next downturn.[14] This can be best described as "value agility," a process where entrepreneurs have to adapt and adjust to continue to meet consumers' perceptions of value your business delivers.[15]

One of the most difficult decisions for a small business owner is whether to stick it out when the economy is in a slump or wave the white flag and close the doors. This is one of the most agonizing decisions for an individual who has spent years, maybe even decades, building a busi-ness from scratch. A key factor would be the age of the owner who does not have a succession plan in place. For example, a business owner in his or her sixties may be better off financially and psychologically to sell the business at whatever price the market will bear and then use his/her expertise as a consultant to help young entrepreneurs create a sound busi-ness plan.[16] Another strategy could be making a long-term key employ-ee(s) partners with the goal of selling them the business eventually. Or the business owner could sell the company to the employees. Employee own-ership could inject new energy—and ideas—into the business. It should go without saying that small business owners need to monitor the pulse of the economy and have contingency plans in place as the economy goes through the business cycle.

The optimal time to sell a small business would be at the peak of the business cycle. This is easier said than done. Needless to say, a profit-able business with a strong consumer base would allow the small business owner to "cash out" and never look back. Depending on the size of the business and the financial resources of one or more key employees who may be the potential buyer, the small business owner could hold "paper" at an interest rate lower than what a bank would charge allowing the new owners to reduce the debt service of their purchase. There are many creative ways for a business owner to cash out when the time is right.[17] Timing the sale of the small business thus maybe one of the most import-ant decisions an entrepreneur would make. An exit strategy, therefore, should be planned in advance in order to avoid making a hasty, unwise, and potentially financially unsound decision.

The Skyscraper Curse, Real Estate Bubbles, and Picking Up the Pieces

The economics and regulatory policies of big cities have made it more difficult for small businesses to survive and thrive. Big city economies—New York, Chicago, Boston, San Francisco, Atlanta, and other major urban centers—have one thread in common; they are also major financial centers, which are the earliest recipients of the Federal Reserve's easy money policies. In other words, the boom phase of the business cycle will be especially strong in these urban hubs and their surrounding suburbs.

As the new money enters the economy in these metropolitan regions, prices tend to rise. For small businesses, that means competing in an economic environment where costs such as wages, rents, and other expenses rise faster than in outlying areas. If small businesses can raise their prices to cover their highest costs, then their profit margins should not be negatively affected. However, if small business' prices tend to be relatively inelastic, then they will have to absorb the higher costs that they will face during boom phase of the cycle.

Small business owners also have to deal with local and state regulations that may raise their costs, which may be difficult if not impossible to pass on to their customers. The pandemic of 2020 further exacerbated small business owners who were locked down for months at a time and then only allowed to open at limited capacity.

For more than 100 years of business cycles, the so-called skyscraper curse has been observed. The "curse" shows the correlation between the building of skyscrapers and the end of the business cycle boom. The explanation is quite straightforward, namely, the Federal Reserve's easy money policies drive down interest rates, which make these projects feasible.[18]

Small businesses may locate in the retail portion of a skyscraper or in surrounding storefronts on pricey streets such as Manhattan's Fifth Avenue, Chicago's Loop, or any other domestic or international city that has had a skyscraper constructed over the decades. The small business owner is in effect speculating that locating near the skyscraper will provide sustainable revenue—and profits. However, when the bust phase of the cycle begins, small business owners may experience the negative consequences of being located in or around an "overbuilt" commercial building.

Although the suburbs generally do not have skyscrapers because of zoning laws and the impracticality of locating such a building outside of a city, real estate bubbles popped in commercial properties and residential housing during the great recession of 2008.[19]

As we have previously mentioned, the old adage regarding stocks is buy low and sell high—or, as Warren Buffett explained the tops and bottoms of prices during the business cycle, "Be fearful when people are greedy and be greedy when people are fearful." This applies to the real estate market as well when prices declined during the bust phase of the cycle and savvy investors were either cash buyers or had access to funds and picked up quality properties at a fraction of their boom phase peak. Investors who snatched up properties when the real estate trust index hit 80 have seen property prices in general quadruple before the pandemic correction caused prices to slide. With short-term interest rates remaining low but long-term rates starting to rise at the beginning of 2021, the boom phase of this cycle could last a few more years. Time will tell if the upswing in prices that have occurred since the panic low in early 2020 is the beginning of a multiyear boom or just a temporary blip.

Location, Location, Location

Is there a best or optimal location for small business? For retail businesses that require foot traffic the answer is absolutely yes. However, with the boom in e-commerce, online sales are becoming an integral component of a small business' operations. Nevertheless, location is critical for retailing or a hospitality business; a poor location could be the death knell for a restaurant or boutique but not so important for a manufacturer, whose customers rarely have to visit the plant. The same goes for a wholesaling operation.[20]

The pandemic has caused some businesses to reinvent themselves or see an opportunity to take a product or service to customers. Monica Pidhorecki lost her job when the tavern where she worked (in Northern New Jersey) shutdown due to COVID-19. Now she is known as the Ice

Cream Lady, serving ice cream from her truck and acknowledging, "This is the best job I've ever had."[21] Established businesses also have taken the truck route in order to sell their products directly to customers given the limited capacity allowed in stores and restaurants. In short, human ingenuity and flexibility have made small business owners resilient in the face of the pandemic.

Surviving and Thriving, Growing the Business, and Preserving Wealth

The business cycle is not going away anytime soon because the Federal Reserve tries to manage the economy by manipulating interest rates and thus creates distortions and unsustainable economic activity. Everybody loves an economic boom because jobs are plentiful, sales are robust, and profits are rising. But when the day of reckoning occurs (when the Fed "tightens" credit conditions to cool off an overheated economy) unemployment increases. At that time, growing—let alone maintaining—revenues is a challenge, and profits will tend to shrink or turn into losses. This is not to say that all businesses—large and small—are affected similarly. That is why it is important for small business owners to have an accurate perspective of the big picture and the possible consequences of the business cycle on their companies.

First and foremost, a small business must have adequate cash reserves throughout the business cycle to meet any contingency plans, especially when the downturn unfolds. By having adequate liquidity, a small business would be able to meet its current expenses including any debt service, during a 12-month or longer recession, which has been the average downturn in the postwar period. In addition, reducing expenses would be an essential tactic to get through a recession relatively intact. As the recession is winding down, small business owners could be in a very strategic position by purchasing assets—inventory, machinery, and so on—from competitors who are liquidating their businesses. Thus, keeping tabs on competitors during the economic downturn would be a worthwhile endeavor that would help a small business thrive during the next upturn in the economy.

There are many great success stories that occurred during the pandemic on how companies adapted and pivoted to meet the needs of customers.

One such company is Eden Park Illumination, Inc. of Champaign, Illinois. Before the pandemic its one product was an ultraviolet (UV) diamond detector technology. The company rapidly shifted its production to a UV light application that would disinfect crowded spaces. By so doing, it added a dozen workers to its 10-person company.[22] The takeaways from the *Wall Street Journal* Small Business Survival Guide (August 1–2, 2020) in light of the pandemic are that health-oriented small businesses survived and thrived: "Focus on what sells, Stay focused on what you know, Go digital, All hands on deck, Get simpler, and go small."[23] Needless to say, funds from the Paycheck Protection Program helped some of the companies profiled refocus their businesses to continue operations.

Small business entrepreneurs can grow their sales and profitability by staying focused on their customers' needs and working with them during a bust phase of the cycle or when an exogenous factor rocks the economy, such as the pandemic did in 2020 and into early 2021. Entrepreneurial empathy will pay huge dividends for small business owners no matter what phase of the business cycle the economy is in or whether the economy is fully opened or in a partial lockdown.

Several common-sense actions would assist small business entrepreneurs to grow the business in a cost-effective way such as maximizing social media, building an effective team, and attending networking events, among other activities.[24]

Even before a small business becomes cash flow positive, the owner should purchase the appropriate insurance policies to protect the company's assets from any potential lawsuit that could be financially devastating.[25] Without adequate insurance, the small business owner can see his years of investment in time, energy, and financial resources virtually disappear from a calamitous lawsuit.

Avoiding the Bubble Fallout

To avoid being a casualty when a financial bubble bursts, a small business—especially a start-up or one in its early stages—should not be highly leveraged. For example, it should not have taken on a substantial amount of debt during the so-called good times. If a small business has a reasonable amount of debt and can cover the interest expense as the economy falters, it should be able to bounce back strongly—and provide breathing room to grow the business during the next upswing in the economy. On the other hand, one of the best strategies for a small business owner is to rely on equity instead of debt in the company's early stages to avoid the burden of interest expenses during a recession.

Creativity, flexibility, ingenuity, insight, and perseverance will help entrepreneurs navigate the business cycle and other disruptions to the economy that make it possible for small business owners to "to fight another day." The entrepreneurs who survived the great recession and were able to reinvent, in some cases, their existing businesses as the bubble was bursting reveal the resiliency of American entrepreneurs. In addition, the small business owners who faced enormous challenges during the pandemic and were able to restructure their businesses to meet the needs of customers once again demonstrate that "necessity is the mother of invention."

Both the Great Recession and the pandemic of 2020 unfortunately caused many small businesses to close their doors forever, dashing the hopes and dreams of long-time business owners, newly arrived immigrants, and women and minority entrepreneurs.[26]

One of the conclusions from the pandemic is that many restaurants and foodservice businesses have poor business models—low margin, high labor costs, insufficient digitization, insufficient insulation from competition, poor cost control, and inadequate cash reserves.

Recessions and pandemics have caused incredible challenges for small business owners. However, we have enough examples of how many of them have weathered the storms that small business owners should take note. Every crisis, if prepared, is an opportunity to apply sound business practices outlined in this chapter.

CHAPTER 9

International Cyclical Impacts on Multinationals and Small Businesses

To set the stage for understanding cyclical developments around the world, we have seen in Chapter 2 that the U.S. economy has experienced recurring business cycles since the early days of the republic. Before the Federal Reserve was created in 1913, banking panics occurred frequently. The cause of 19th-century banking panics is attributed to the fractional reserve banking system, which creates new money that businesses, farmers, and individuals eagerly borrow.[1] Some of the new money was used for speculative purposes, such as land purchases, which drives up the price of many assets including commodities creating an unsustainable boom. As the new money diffuses through the economy and holders want to redeem their banknotes for specie—gold and silver—held in the banks' reserves, lo and behold, the bankers did not have enough "real" money in their vaults. In short, a bank run would ensue, causing some banks to collapse followed by a depression.[2]

This reoccurring phenomenon of money creation, speculation, boom, malinvestments, crisis, and depression did not end with the establishment of the Federal Reserve, which was created for the express purpose of "stabilizing" the economy. For more than 100 years since the Federal Reserve was given the power to create money and manage interest rates, the business cycle has not disappeared. In fact, the historical record is clear. The Federal Reserve has destabilized the economy beginning with the forgotten depression of 1920–1921, created an unsustainable boom in the 1920s, and prolonged the Great Depression of the 1930s.

After World War II, the Federal Reserve continued to create new money and the boom-bust cycles persisted. And more recently "easy

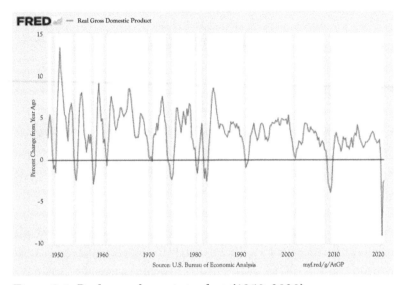

Figure 9.1 Real gross domestic product (1950–2020)

Source: U.S. Bureau of Economic Analysis, Real gross domestic product [GDPC1], retrieved from FRED, Federal Reserve Bank of St. Louis; https://fred.stlouisfed.org/series/GDPC1, February 12, 2021.

money" caused the dot-com and housing bubbles. (Figure 9.1 shows the ups and downs of the U.S. gross domestic product after World War II.)

The so-called everything bubble was well underway before the pandemic of 2020 struck the United States and world economies. The sharp rebound in the U.S. economy in late 2020, including the booming stock market and robust residential real estate price inflation, has reflected the enormous amount of liquidity the Federal Reserve poured into the economy since early 2020.

Prior to the pandemic, there was compelling evidence that the U.S. economy as well as other countries in the Group of Seven (G7) (Canada, U.K., Japan, Germany, France, and Italy) were slowing down or on the cusp of a recession.[3] In other words, it was becoming more evident that the major economies of the world, except China, were in "sync." (See the performance of several of the G7 economies in the following figures: Figure 9.2–Figure 9.7.) The graphs reveal the deceleration in economic activity before the pandemic and the plunge that occurred in 2020 as governments locked down their economies to stop the spread and the subsequent rebounds as restrictions were eased.

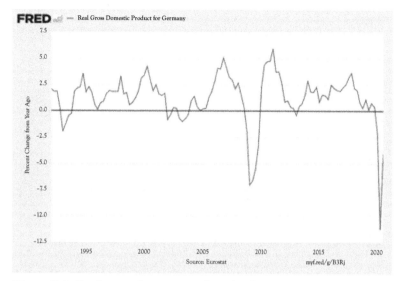

Figure 9.2 Real gross domestic product for Germany

Source: Eurostat, Real gross domestic product for Germany [CLVMNACSCAB1GQDE], retrieved from FRED, Federal Reserve Bank of St. Louis; https://fred.stlouisfed.org/series/CLVMNACS-CAB1GQDE, February 13, 2021. © European Union, 1995–2021

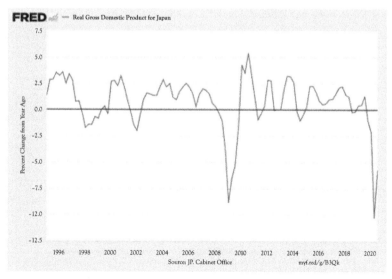

Figure 9.3 Real gross domestic product for Japan

Source: JP. Cabinet Office, Real gross domestic product for Japan [JPNRGDPEXP], retrieved from FRED, Federal Reserve Bank of St. Louis; https://fred.stlouisfed.org/series/JPNRGDPEXP, February 12, 2021.

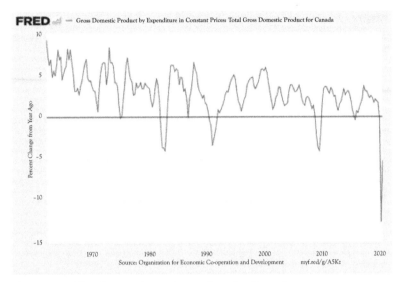

Figure 9.4 Total gross domestic product for Canada

Source: Organization for Economic Co-operation and Development, Gross domestic product by expenditure in constant prices: Total gross domestic product for Canada [NAEXKP01CAQ189S], retrieved from FRED, Federal Reserve Bank of St. Louis; https://fred.stlouisfed.org/series/NAEXK-P01CAQ189S, February 12, 2021.

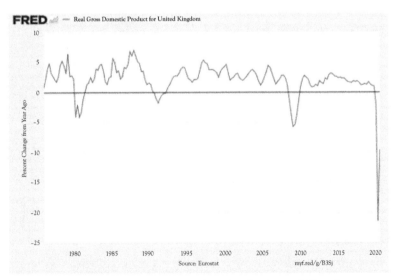

Figure 9.5 Real gross domestic product for the United Kingdom

Source: Eurostat, Real gross domestic product for the United Kingdom [CLVMNACSCAB 1GQUK], retrieved from FRED, Federal Reserve Bank of St. Louis; https://fred.stlouisfed.org/series/CLVMNACSCAB1GQUK, February 12, 2021. Copyright, European Union, http://ec.europa.eu, 1995–2016.

Figure 9.6 Total gross domestic product for Mexico

Source: Organization for Economic Co-operation and Development, Gross domestic product by expenditure in constant prices: Total gross domestic product for Mexico [NAEXKP01MXQ189S], retrieved from FRED, Federal Reserve Bank of St. Louis; https://fred.stlouisfed.org/series/NAEXKP01MXQ189S, February 13, 2021.

At the regional level, the United States, Canada, and Mexico, which are interlinked because of geography and/or culture, have had highly correlated business cycles in recent years. (See Figure 9.6 for Mexican economic performance.) Monetary policy in all three countries tends to be synchronous, which would prevent capital from flowing into one country at the expense of other countries in the trading bloc. The three North American countries have seen their business cycles become more correlated.[4]

International capital flows created bubble conditions in Mexico, Thailand, Iceland, and other emerging markets in the 1990s; the culprit was not surprising, easy money conditions in the United States and other developed economies provided the wherewithal for banks to lend what was thought to be extraordinary profit opportunities in these countries.[5] As Aliber and Kindleberger observed:

> The uniqueness of the last forty years is that there have been four waves of financial crises; each wave was preceded by a surge in the supplies of credit that involve three, four, or in some episodes eight or ten countries.[6]

The authors' summary of the first (1970s) of the four waves includes Mexico, Brazil, and Argentina and other developing countries that borrowed heavily from Western banks that increased to unsustainable levels. The second wave unfolded in the 1980s, and is highlighted by "the mother of all asset price bubbles" in Tokyo as the supply of credit soared after bank regulations were eased.[7] Investment inflows to emerging economies in Brazil, Argentina, Thailand, Malaysia, and others set the stage for the third wave, the 1990s financial crises.[8] In the early 2000s, the fourth wave occurred when real estate bubbles unfolded in the United States, Britain, Spain, Ireland, and Iceland, among other countries, after another episode of easy credit made it possible for residential home buyers and purchasers of commercial real estate to bid up prices to unsustainable levels.[9]

Financial crises have occurred throughout the world for the past 400 years, mostly confined to one country or region. The events of the past 100 years reveal how crises have been more synchronous since the Great Depression of the 1930s. But even more fascinating is how the major industrial economies are virtually lockstep as their economies boom and bust together. This is not surprising given the similar policies of central bankers in North America, Europe, and Japan—namely, keep interest rates low and create money to boost output and employment. However, the evidence shows that these policies are counterproductive. The economic fluctuations since the mid-1990s continue with the downturns being more severe and unsettling for businesses of all sizes and workers.

Nevertheless, corporate managers who oversee tens or hundreds of millions or possibly billions of dollars of assets and small-business owners who serve their local and/or regional markets, they can survive and thrive despite the business cycle. The next two sections will focus on how decision makers in large-scale businesses or mom-and-pop shops can be better prepared to navigate the inevitable economic fluctuations that have become more internationally synchronized.

Opportunities for Multinationals

Trade is the lifeblood of civilization. Domestically, local and interregional trade creates a network of mutually beneficial relationships between buyers and sellers to achieve their goals. In cities and towns across America, shops located on Main Street and in a multitude of neighborhoods throughout a metropolitan area, entrepreneurs provide goods and services that satisfy the wants and needs of consumers. In addition, consumers benefit from trading with merchants across the national economic landscape. Supermarkets and grocery stores, for example, sell fruits, vegetables, and meat products that are shipped from farms and cattle ranches that are located hundreds if not a couple thousand miles away for consumers in the northeast and upper Midwest. Economic specialization, therefore, increases living standards by allowing entrepreneurs to provide the marketplace with products and services that consumers want.

International trade allows specialization to occur across the globe. For the United States, this means nearly $5 trillion of goods and services were imported and exported in 2020. Both imports ($2.81 trillion) and exports ($2.13 trillion) declined in 2020 because of the global pandemic, creating a trade deficit of $678.7 billion, an increase from 2019, when the deficit was $616.8 billion.[10] In addition, when all the numbers are tallied for 2020, global trade probably contracted by 8 percent, but may rebound to prepandemic levels in 2021.[11]

Despite the challenges entrepreneurs around the world faced during 2020 because of the pandemic, there are nevertheless compelling reasons for U.S. businesses to export their goods and services to the rest of the world. The most obvious reason is that 95 percent of the world's consumers reside outside United States and have 84 percent of global spending power.[12]

Major benefits for both small and large businesses that export include higher productivity. According to data compiled by the U.S. Census Bureau and the U.S. international trade commission, businesses with less than 250 employees had nearly two times more revenue than nonexporting firms, and generated 70 percent more revenue per employee.[13] Additional research concluded that workers earn more in industries where exports are a major component of the local economy; exporting firms tend to have higher revenues, faster revenue growth, and higher labor productivity. Lastly, according to one academic study, "exporters file seven times MORE patents and deliver four times MORE product innovations than their non-exporting peers."[14] The overwhelming evidence is undeniable—no matter what, the size of the firm exporting is a pathway for substantial business success.

However, trade throughout the world is less "free" than it otherwise would be because of the confluence of several factors. Countries use various policies to boost and/or hinder trade such as quotas, tariffs, subsidies, foreign exchange manipulation, and taxes—among other tools—to manage imports and exports. Managed trade creates "winners and losers" such as consumers who have to pay higher prices for imports, importers who may see their supply chain disrupted, workers who may lose their jobs, and companies that may see their revenue decline because of interventionist trade policies. Apparent winners from managed trade include domestic companies whose overseas competitors may ship fewer goods to the United States because of tariffs and/or quotas—and thus would be able to raise their prices. Workers in so-called protected industries may have their wages raised as the firms they are working in expand and need to attract more workers. On the other hand, if companies that are hurt by protectionist measures have to lay off workers or shut their doors, the unemployed workers may depress wages in industries that presumably are supposed to be the beneficiaries of higher tariffs, and so forth.

Managed trade has many unintended consequences. Nevertheless, businesses have to keep their eyes on the prize, which is creating value in the marketplace, both domestically and possibly internationally.

The trade war with China that began during the Trump administration has rattled American businesses. Both importers and exporters have had to deal with another contentious factor in doing business with America's largest trading partner. In fact, one consequence from the trade tensions with China and the pandemic is the shift in direct foreign investment from the United States to China.[15] Foreign direct investment (FDI) in the United States has been declining since 2016, when it peaked at $472 billion. China, meanwhile, has attracted FDI as a strategic policy to provide employment for its massive labor force, and its ability to remain relatively open during the pandemic.[16] China's growing GDP is illustrated in Figure 9.7.

U.S. companies that have been in China or even thinking of entering the Mainland may want to follow the suggestions of David Nordstrom, the chairman of consulting firm PRI, and John Evans, managing partner of Tractus Asia. Their advice was recently reported by Robert Hess,

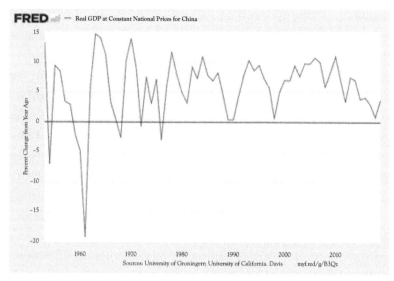

Figure 9.7 Historical real GDP at constant national prices for China

Source: University of Groningen and University of California, Davis, Real GDP at Constant National Prices for China [RGDPNACNA666NRUG], retrieved from FRED, Federal Reserve Bank of St. Louis; https://fred.stlouisfed.org/series/RGDPNACNA666NRUG, February 12, 2021.

vice chairman of Newmark Knight Frank, in his summary of Nordstrom's and Evans' presentation about the Chinese market.[17] Needless to say, the suggestions are what you would expect—they range from sourcing the materials outside of China to making products for the Chinese market and non-U.S. markets as well as negotiating better terms from Chinese suppliers and other tactical and strategic initiatives to maintain a presence in China and overseas locations.[18]

One of the most successful U.S. multinationals that has grown into an international "behemoth," Estée Lauder, began as a New York–based cosmetic company in the 1930s whose founder was "a genius at sales," according to 87-year-old Leonard Lauder, son of Mrs. Lauder.[19] Lauder recounts how the company went from less than $1 million in sales (1958) to more than $14 billion in revenue in 2020, and is now worth more than $107 billion (February 2021), making the Lauder family one of the wealthiest in America.

Lauder took the company global and its 25 brands are now sold in 150 countries. According to Lauder, "We were one of the first companies to enter the Asian market. If you're the first to market, you always win."[20] Lauder hopes his book (published in November 2020) is an inspiration to anyone who is willing to work, persevere, and be optimistic about the future so they can achieve great success just as the company his mother founded in the midst of the Great Depression.[21]

The bottom line for multinationals could not be clearer. Knowing the economic, financial, political, and cultural landscapes of overseas markets and having a product(s) or service(s) that will be in demand plus having all of the key personnel in place makes for a successful formula to penetrate non-U.S. markets. The growth and success of Estée Lauder since the Great Depression occurred despite World War II and the numerous boom and bust cycles since the economic calamity of the 1930s. Nevertheless, companies with more economically sensitive products or services should be able to survive and thrive during the boom-bust cycle by implementing the tactics and strategies outlined in previous chapters. If business is about "survival of the fittest," corporate managers and small-business owners who are best able to identify the coming peak of the boom and take necessary actions to limit the "damage" during the bust will continue to prosper in the years and decades ahead.

Small Business Opportunities

Just as adults once were infants and youngsters, large businesses were once small businesses that may have started in someone's basement, on a dining room table, or in a garage. As a small business grows, over time it may become a "behemoth" like Apple, Microsoft, Netflix, Amazon, Facebook, Tesla, and scores of other businesses that operate around the world. The common thread of all these businesses is the vision of their founders and their focus on the long-term sustainability of their firm with products and services for the masses. Another entrepreneur who could be added to the above list is Warren Buffett, CEO of Berkshire Hathaway since 1965. Buffett took an $11 million declining New England textile company and turned it into a $500 billion conglomerate nearly 60 years later. Buffett's genius was not that he had a product or service to sell to the masses, but that he was the "great allocator" of capital that allowed him to purchase companies such as GEICO, Dairy Queen, Benjamin Moore, Fruit of the Loom, Duracell, See's Candies, and other businesses in a variety of industries.[22] Berkshire owns a $275 billion portfolio of stocks including Apple,

Coca-Cola, American Express, and dozens of quality companies, including foreign businesses.[23]

For Warren Buffett, the secret of his success was realizing that compounding money over the long term would lead to wealth and possibly great wealth, a lesson he learned when he was 10 years old.[24] As Jason Zweig points out in his summary of Buffett's investment philosophy, "Even at low to moderate rates of return, long periods of continuous growth turn small amounts into mountains of money." Warren Buffett's long-term perspective has paid off for him and his shareholders, whom he calls partners. Berkshire's stock has increased by more than 2.7 million percent since 1964 or more than 20 percent compounded annually, while the S&P 500 has increased slightly—nearly 20,000 percent, or about 10 percent compounded annually. In addition, the price of Berkshire Hathaway stock has declined by about 50 percent four times during Buffett's helm as CEO. This did not faze Buffett at all. The following chart (Figure 9.8) shows the decline of Berkshire's stock price both during the dot-com bubble burst and the housing bubble bust. Despite these "setbacks" over the long term, the stock price of quality businesses will be much higher than the day when the stock is purchased. As of March 2021, Berkshire's stock rose above $400,000 for the first time.

Small business owners are in many respects in the same position Warren Buffett was in when he took over Berkshire in 1964. Buffett did not have to start from scratch, but his challenge was how to use the assets of Berkshire to generate shareholder wealth. Buffett successfully utilized the investment skills he learned as graduate student of the father of value investing, Benjamin Graham at Columbia University, to become the "world's greatest investor." Buffett, however, does not consider himself an "investor," but an entrepreneur who takes a very long-term view of business. The same mindset could be said for Jeff Bezos, the late Steve Jobs, Reed Hastings, and Elon Musk, who are (or were) not focused on short-term profits but on creating value for customers.

To tap into the international markets, where most of the world's customers live, U.S. small business owners can begin by obtaining tools that are available from the federal government, such as *Ten Free Tools to Help You Become an Expert in Exporting*.[25] In addition, small business owners should take advantage of the information available in the Office of the U.S. Trade

BRK/A Berkshire Hathway, Inc. NYSE
30-Mar-2021 3:54pm
— BRK/A (Monthly) 389835.00

Open 372555.00 High 407750.00 Low 368430.00 Last 389835.00 Volume 54.4K Chg +25255.00 (+6.93%) ▲

©StockCharts.com

Figure 9.8 Performance of Berkshire Hathaway stock (1995–2021)

Courtesy of Stockcharts.com

Representative, which contains the terms of free trade agreements and other international protocols to facilitate trade around the world.[26]

There are enormous opportunities for small businesses to export their goods and provide their services to scores of countries around the world despite the boom-bust cycles, which have become more synchronous. That could work to a small business' advantage. Booms tend to last longer than busts and therefore small business owners who keep their finger on the pulse of business conditions are in a strategic position to ride the wave of the boom and take appropriate measures when the economy begins to slow down. When the bust occurs that is when small business owners can gobble up assets at depressed prices to ride the wave of the next boom.

Although the major economies of the world probably are more in "synch" than ever before, as the boom-bust cycle has linked the U.S. economy with many of our trading partners, small businesses should have an advantage over large corporations to deal with deteriorating economic conditions. Small business owners should be able to adjust their plans quickly when the bust is on the horizon, especially if they have a set of "what if" scenarios they could choose from to implement a "survival" strategy. Of course, if corporate managers also employ the tactics and strategies outlined here, they too would survive—and thrive—as the boom-bust cycle unfolds.

Over the long term, small business owners will be able to take their one-million-dollar-or-more business to a level of great success as long as they have a niche in the marketplace and, as Buffett would like to say, a large "moat" to keep their competitors at bay.

CHAPTER 10

Future Economic Trends: Innovators, Disruption, Cycles, and the Threat of Stagnation

The old adage, "If a tree falls in the forest and no one was there to hear it, does it make a sound?" can also be applied to business. If an individual has invented a new product or has an idea for new service but does not have capital to bring it to the marketplace, is it really a breakthrough?

A key component in taking a product or idea to the marketplace is private equity—namely, the pooling of funds from major firms such as the Blackstone Group, Kohlberg Kravis Roberts, the Carlyle Group, or dozens of other private equity outfits and/or from very high net worth individuals who take part ownership in a new venture. These funds make it possible for a start-up to invest in capital equipment, software, R&D, and hiring key personnel. If the new product or service has a successful "incubation" period, then the company may go public with an IPO—an initial public offering—to raise additional funds from the general public and institutional investors.

In recent years, private equity has been very active in buying the songbooks of major artists such as Bob Dylan and Taylor Swift, allowing these artists to "cash out" this valuable asset. However, David Stockman, former director of the Office of Management and Budget during the Reagan administration, points out how private equity firms such as Bain Capital rode the financial bubble to great profits by loading up companies with debt, "cashing out" and leaving shareholders holding the bag.[1] Private equity, therefore, was criticized for hollowing out companies at the expense of employee, shareholders, and local economies.

Nevertheless, private equity plays an enormous role in the U.S. economy, creating value for consumers, employing millions of U.S. workers, and increasing wealth for pension plans and other institutional investors.[2] Smith and Earle cite a report issued by Ernst & Young revealing widespread economic impact of private equity-controlled firms, such as employing eight million workers who are on an average salary of $71,000 annually. These firms also generated more than $1 trillion in account activity in 2018.[3]

During the 2020 pandemic, despite the private equity investment ($708.4 billion), the number of deals (5,309) declined—not unexpectedly —from a year earlier. It was the first annual drop since 2009, as the first half of the year put a lot of deals on hold.[4] However, as 2020 unfolded, private equity deals picked up steam as the year drew to a close. And as we shall see below, private equity has been funding the "disruptors," start-ups that have been in the vanguard of the latest generation of innovators who have been creating solutions in virtually every sector of the economy.

Innovation will cause disruption in businesses where new processes are created to challenge long-established firms. For example, technology is one area that has caused a major disruption in how people get their news. Newspapers were completely derailed and disrupted from this outside force. If you plan to be a disruptor, then you are more likely to be prepared for when a disruption comes into your own business and impacts the way your customers perceive the product or service. Private equity allows entrepreneurs to figure out ways to upend the status quo and conduct processes and tasks in a new manner.

Innovator and disruptor Elon Musk has established a new way of thinking in education by disregarding grades or set class structures. In 2014, he opened a nonprofit school at SpaceX headquarters with these new ways of learning and allowed students to even opt out of subjects they do not enjoy. To be a disruptor in business and in society, one needs to look for inspiration even in the most unlikely of places. Often humans fear change when they should embrace it and be preparing for the next upheaval, whether in business models or the consumer market. Even Deloitte reported that "90% of managers and executives surveyed said that they expect technology to disrupt their industries" but less than half said they are prepared for it. This shows that many entrepreneurs know they need to prep for change, but they struggle to become prepared.[5]

Since 2013, cable channel CNBC has compiled an annual Disruptor 50 list which it announces every June. For the past eight years, 58 other companies went public via an IPO (Peloton, Casper, and DoorDash, to name a few of the recent start-ups that have gone public) or by direct listing. Large companies such as Facebook, Alphabet, Microsoft, Verizon, and American Express have acquired one or more of the 33 companies that were on the list. Not surprisingly, eight companies fell by the wayside.[6]

The start-ups on the 2020 list include disruptors in higher education, e-commerce, cosmetics, language instruction, warehousing, trucking logistics, and in virtually every sector of the financial world. Thirty-six of the companies have already passed on the billion-dollar market valuation, and have raised $74 billion in private equity, implying that all 50 companies have a total market valuation of $277 billion. In addition, 37 companies have hired new employees because of the increased demand for their products or services as the pandemic unfolded.[7]

The companies that have made it onto the Disruptor 50 list are a reflection of human ingenuity that continues despite business cycles, financial bubbles, burdensome regulations, and shifting tax policies, which have affected to some degree the firms' revenues and profitability. Nevertheless, disruptors have proven to be resilient and successful for longer than the eight years CNBC has been compiling its list. Companies such as Amazon, Netflix, and dozens more are changing the business landscape and by doing so improving living standards for the vast majority of Americans. This will confirm Warren Buffett's insight that the best days of America are still ahead.

Business Cycles as Far as the Eye Can See?

As we have seen in Chapter 2, the U.S. economy has had booms and busts since its founding. In the 19th century, banking panics occurred periodically because the banks created more banknotes than the gold and silver they had in reserve thus creating an unsustainable boom in their communities. When depositors became concerned about the solvency of their local banks, they attempted to redeem the banknotes for "specie" and if they were lucky enough to be the first in line, they got "real money" in exchange for their paper banknotes. Latecomers to the banks would get a percentage for their banknotes or nothing at all.

When it was founded in 1913, the mission of the Federal Reserve was to "smooth out" the business cycle, maintain the purchasing power of the dollar, and end bank runs by becoming the "lender of last resort." The evidence is clear: the business cycle has not been dampened, the dollar's purchasing power has declined by 95 percent since 1913, but the Fed has injected "liquidity" into the financial sector to prop up banks and other institutions. In other words, the Fed has the "backs" of the bankers.

Despite the Fed's failure to create a sustainable economy, its mission has shifted over the years and now is focused on targeting the consumer price inflation rate to 2 percent annually and promoting "full employment." In other words, the Federal Reserve's primary tool—targeting short-term interest rates, the so-called Fed funds rate—to achieve its goals has caused another set of distortions and dislocations in recent years, massive financial bubbles in the stock market and real estate.

After the Great Recession (2007–2009), the so-called everything bubble began lifting stock prices and other assets to frothy levels. The pandemic of 2020 caused the shortest and swiftest drop in the stock market from February to March, and the subsequent boom in the stock market and real estate prices reflected the enormous amount of liquidity the Federal Reserve created (Figure 10.1) to prop up the economy as both short-term and long-term interest rates declined markedly (Figure 10.2 and Figure 10.3).

As governors and mayors locked down their economies and the unemployment rate soared (Figure 10.4), federal spending increased dramatically (Figure 10.5), and the federal budget deficit skyrocketed (Figure 10.6). Policy makers used all the tools at their disposal to make up for lost income of individuals and businesses and to keep rates low to "stimulate" spending and investment. Although the economy has rebounded from its pandemic lows, there is growing evidence that consumer price inflation will accelerate, which is not surprising given the 25 percent increase in the money supply in 2020 (Figure 10.7). Money supply growth always precedes price inflation.

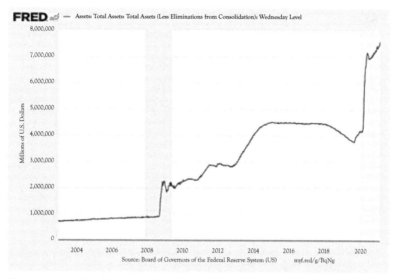

Figure 10.1 Total assets (less eliminations from consolidation)

Source: Board of Governors of the Federal Reserve System (U.S.), Assets: Total assets: Total assets (less eliminations from consolidation): Wednesday level [WALCL], retrieved from FRED, Federal Reserve Bank of St. Louis; https://fred.stlouisfed.org/series/WALCL, March 01, 2021.

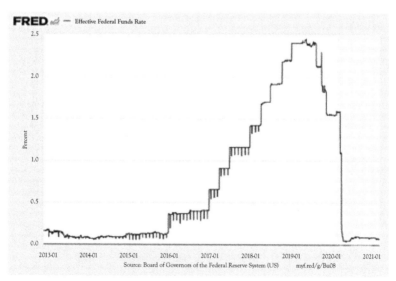

Figure 10.2 Effective federal funds rate

Source: Board of Governors of the Federal Reserve System (U.S.), Effective Federal funds rate [DFF], retrieved from FRED, Federal Reserve Bank of St. Louis; https://fred.stlouisfed.org/series/DFF, March 01, 2021.

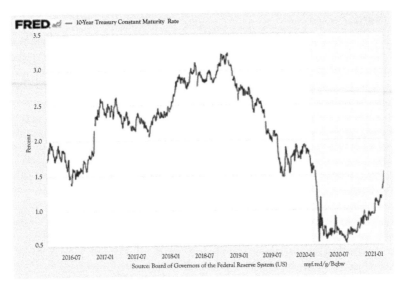

Figure 10.3 Ten-year treasury constant maturity rate

Source: Board of Governors of the Federal Reserve System (U.S.), 10-year treasury constant maturity rate [DGS10], retrieved from FRED, Federal Reserve Bank of St. Louis; https://fred.stlouisfed .org/series/DGS10, March 01, 2021.

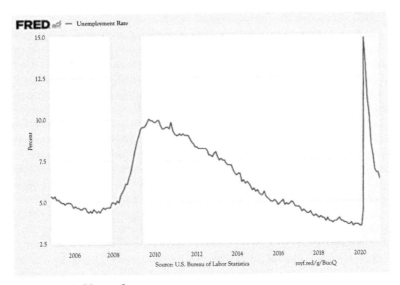

Figure 10.4 Unemployment rate

Source: U.S. Bureau of Labor Statistics, Unemployment rate [UNRATE], retrieved from FRED, Federal Reserve Bank of St. Louis; https://fred.stlouisfed.org/series/UNRATE, March 01, 2021.

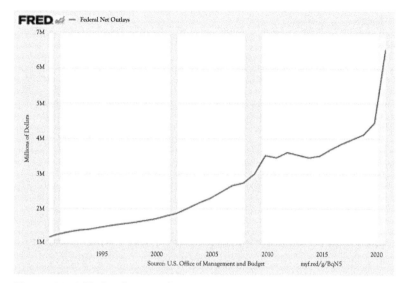

Figure 10.5 Federal net outlays

Source: U.S. Office of Management and Budget, Federal net outlays [FYONET], retrieved from FRED, Federal Reserve Bank of St. Louis; https://fred.stlouisfed.org/series/FYONET, March 01, 2021.

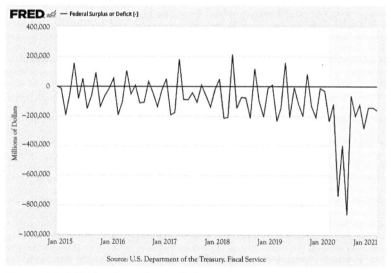

Figure 10.6 Federal surplus or deficit

Source: U.S. Office of Management and Budget, Federal Surplus or Deficit [-] [FYFSD], retrieved from FRED, Federal Reserve Bank of St. Louis; https://fred.stlouisfed.org/series/FYFSD, March 01, 2021.

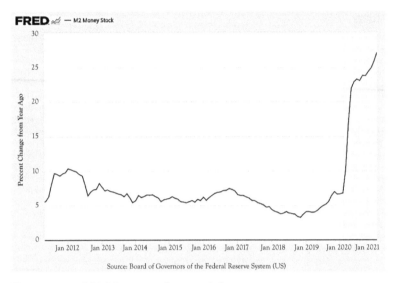

Figure 10.7 M2 Money stock rate of change

Board of Governors of the Federal Reserve System (US), M2 Money Stock [M2SL], retrieved from
FRED, Federal Reserve Bank of St. Louis; https://fred.stlouisfed.org/series/M2SL, March 30, 2021.

There are several scenarios besides higher consumer and producer
prices in years ahead. The last episodes of higher inflation (1970s) were
also known as the "lost decade" because the unemployment rate remained
relatively high, the economy was buffeted by recessions, and real economic growth was erratic (Figure 10.8).

The stagflation scenario is based on the assumption that low short-
term interest rates, which the Fed announced it would maintain until its
inflation and unemployment targets are met, would not produce a robust
recovery but higher prices and a subpar economy.[8] In other words, if the
Fed tries to "normalize" interest rates, an economic downturn would follow, which would cause it to reverse course and pump liquidity into the
economy. Hence, stop-and-go monetary policy would give us the worst
of worlds—higher inflation and recession: stagflation.

Another (ominous) scenario that was beginning to be discussed in
early 2021 was the possibility of hyperinflation in the United States.
Hyperinflation is typically defined as a period when prices are rising 50
percent or *more per month*. Something as inconceivable as runaway inflation in the United States would occur, and the Federal Reserve may have
already planted the seeds of such a scenario in 2020.

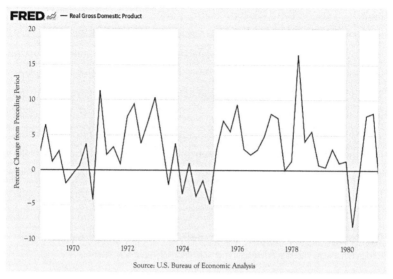

Figure 10.8 Real gross domestic product rate of change

Source: U.S. Bureau of Economic Analysis, Real Gross Domestic Product [A191RL1Q225SBEA], retrieved from FRED, Federal Reserve Bank of St. Louis; https://fred.stlouisfed.org/series/ A191RL1Q225SBEA, March 01, 2021.

Although the rate of consumer price inflation has been tepid for more than 20 years, the historic increase and the money supply in 2020 could be a harbinger of how the Federal Reserve would react to a major stock market meltdown and/or economic implosion. The Fed's unprecedented money printing in 2020 reveals how it may react if stock market fell off the cliff … again, and the unemployment rate skyrocketed … again.

One of the key factors in a hyperinflation scenario is when the so-called velocity of money increases exponentially as people want to exchange their cash and checkbook money rapidly before it becomes worth less and less as the central bank floods the economy with new money to prop up economic activity.[9] In other words, a hyperinflation scenario would unfold if the Federal Reserve throws caution to the wind and floods the economy with an extraordinary amount of new money and people spend it like a "hot potato" to avoid losing the purchasing power of their dollar holdings.

Can hyperinflation happen in America? It already has. Inflation occurred during the Revolutionary War when the Continental Congress authorized the printing of money to pay for the supplies needed to fight the British and pay the soldiers.[10] During the Civil War, the South printed money to pay for its secession effort and caused hyperinflation.[11]

So the real question is: can hyperinflation happen again? If foreign holders of dollars decide to swap them for other currencies, gold, crypto currency, and other assets, the value of the dollar would decline precipitously on foreign exchange markets. Thus, one of the leading indicators of a hyperinflation scenario would be the action of dollar holders around the world. If a "run" on the dollar unfolds, the Fed could buy up dollars with gold and other "hard assets" on its balance sheet or borrow foreign currencies from the U.S. Treasury to stem the collapse of the greenback's value. But with trillions of dollars and U.S. government securities held overseas, a run on the dollar like a massive tsunami coming ashore would be devastating to the American people holding dollars.

In short, the U.S. economy could be on the precipice of a hyperinflation scenario. There is one sure way to prevent such a phenomenon and that would be for the Federal Reserve to stop printing money and allow the marketplace to set interest rates and prices. Unfortunately, the groupthink at the Fed still clings to the notion that the Fed can manage the U.S. economy with impunity for the betterment of society. Both history and theory suggests otherwise. Sustainable prosperity depends upon price discovery and sound money, which can only be accomplished by replacing the Fed's targeting of interest rates and an "unlimited" checking account with a free market money and banking sector. Until that day arrives, we can expect more booms and busts, bubbles, and the possibility of hyperinflation.

Boom to Bust to Stagflation? Is the United States on the Verge of Becoming Japan?

One of the continuing fears of policy makers since the Great Depression is that deflation would occur again causing an implosion in economic activity as sales, investment, prices, and wages collapse producing widespread misery. According to policy makers and most economists, the pain of a deflationary depression thus must be avoided at all costs. But as economists who apply the Austrian theory of the business cycle point out, a deflationary depression is inevitable if the central bank inflates money and credit, which sets into motion an unsustainable boom.[12] The so-called Austrian advice to avoid a depression therefore is for the central bank to refrain from manipulating interest rates below what the free market would fix and cease from creating new money, which inflates asset prices and both consumer and producer prices that will deflate when the bust unfolds.

In a free market, slowly falling prices, that is, deflation, is the "natural" tendency for virtually all prices as the output of goods and services increases as the supply of money is relatively stable. Even as the U.S. economy has experienced virtually higher consumer prices across the board since the 1930s, the prices of some goods and services have declined to reflect the enormous productivity in areas like high-tech (high definition television, computers, and so forth) and Lasik eye surgery—to name some obvious examples of how deflation benefits consumers and thus is a boon to society.[13]

As the pandemic was unfolding in 2020, the financial press began to cite the threat of stagflation—subpar economic growth and rising inflation.[14] That could be one scenario in the cards similar to the Japanese economy experience since its huge bubble burst in 1989. When the Japanese bubble burst, policy makers implemented another round of easy money policies and robust government spending to boost the economy. The result has been three decades of lackluster economic performance and the creation of "zombie" corporations.[15] These corporations are hanging on by a thread only because the central bank is subsidizing them in the form of ultra-low interest rates. In a free market, these corporations would have been liquidated or merged with a financially strong company so their assets could be put to better use.

Could the United States enter an extended period of stagflation with very low short-term interest rates to prop up shaky corporations? This is one of the real possibilities in a postpandemic America. According to economist David Rosenberg, "Stagflation is inevitable," because costs are rising for producers, who in turn will raise prices for customers.[16] In other words, it would be a period of so-called cost-push inflation. In the final analysis, inflation, as Milton Friedman reminded us decades ago, is always a monetary phenomenon; then any price hikes—wages, raw materials, consumer prices, real estate, and so on—are the consequences of the Federal Reserve's creating new money.

Federal government's "stimulus" spending in 2020 and 2021, the Federal Reserve's commitment to keep interest rates low for several years, and the huge money supply increase in 2020 are all the ingredients for stagflation. For both large- and small-sized businesses, their task will be to use the tools outlined in earlier chapters to navigate the ebbs and flows of the economy during what could be a very tumultuous number of years in the 2020s.

Lastly, the so-called graying of the world's population is well underway and the challenges for policy makers cannot be overstated. In addition, the opportunities for businesses are multifaceted. How will countries, especially the United States, deal with the pressures on social security and Medicare benefits promised to America's senior citizens to avoid a reduction in benefits and higher taxes on workers to shore up the system, when the Medicare Trust Fund runs out in 2024 and the Social Security Fund runs out in 2031? And the pandemic's impact on retirees and soon-to-be retirees' plans may have been permanently transformed. Because of the depressed short-term interest rates, many senior citizens have decided to keep working because the return from their savings accounts is virtually negligible and thus their retirement income would be much less than expected.

An aging workforce may be a boon to businesses because older workers take fewer sick days, are more productive, and have more experience than their younger counterparts.[17] Ironically, then, the looming trust fund crises may spark a productivity revival in American businesses. In addition, a major challenge facing America, given the enormous amount of deaths from COVID-19 in nursing homes during the pandemic, is how to provide safe facilities for retirees. One possible entrepreneurial opportunity would be to create small clusters of housing—serving 10 to 20 retirees—instead of nursing homes with dozens of residents.

As we have seen in virtually every sector of the U.S. economy, innovation and ingenuity are ubiquitous to America. If entrepreneurs have the freedom to innovate and are not stymied by unnecessary regulations, we should expect "disruptors" to tackle America's retirement crisis with gusto. Time will tell if America's policy makers will reverse course and not have the economy go down the road Japan has traveled for three decades. Implementing market-oriented policies in the 21st century would avoid the counterproductive stop-and-go policies that undermine sustainable prosperity. American businesses will survive and thrive by continuing to create value for consumers and focusing their attention on changing consumer tastes and preferences. Unfortunately, they may have to deal with future bubbles bursting, as long as policy makers believe they can—and have to—manage the $21 trillion U.S. economy.

Appendix

A. Checklist for opportunities and threats
   a. Corporate actions
      Monitor yield curve at Federal Reserve Economic Data page, https://fred.stlouisfed.org/series/T10Y2Y. Also, see the essay by economist Robert Murphy, https://mises.org/wire/inverted-yield-curve-and-recession.

      Keep close tabs on suppliers. Price increases reveal an inflationary boom is underway, and when the Federal Reserve begins to tighten the money supply and raises the Fed funds rate to prevent price inflation from accelerating, the countdown to the recession begins.

      As the boom is maturing, prepare a list of possible takeovers to purchase assets at discount prices as the recession reaches its depths.

      Monitor final sales closely to determine if consumers are beginning to reduce their demand for your products and/or services. Have plans in place to deal with secular and/or cyclical changes in sales and expenses. Adjust capital expenditures accordingly to reflect long-term prospects.
   b. Small business action
      Follow the guidelines mentioned earlier and pay particular close attention to local and regional business conditions to avoid expanding at the peak of the boom, when economic conditions would soon deteriorate.

      When it appears the recession is ending, such as monthly unemployment numbers have stopped accelerating, the economy would appear to be poised for the next boom phase of the cycle. This could be time to begin expanding to other locations or taking over failed competitors.

B. Websites: taking pulse of the economy

    a. Federal Reserve of St. Louis, https://fred.stlouisfed.org, especially FRED, cited above for popular time series that monitor the economy discussed in the text.

    b. Bureau of Labor Statistics (bls.gov) contains national and local data that could be helpful to monitor economic conditions in your metropolitan area, city, or town.

    c. Opinion and analysis that can be found on scores of websites include, *Bloomberg* (Bloomberg.com), *CNBC* (cnbc.com), *Barron's* (barrons.com), *Wall Street Journal* (wsj.com), Mises.org (mises.org), AIER (aier.org), *Zero Hedge* (zerohedge.com). Scan these websites for essays by economists, investment analysts, and other professionals.

C. Books and essays

    a. A comprehensive library of books on economics and public, many of which are available as PDFs can be found at https://mises.org/books-library. Other worthwhile books and essays are available at https:// independent.org/publications/, https://aier.org/articles/, and material from scores of other organizations that can be obtained by Googling economic research for diverse perspectives on the economy.

Notes

Chapter 1

1. "SWOT Analysis: How to Develop a Strategy for Success." (n.d.).
2. Ovidijus (February 13, 2013).
3. DeFranco (2015).
4. Rothbard (1970).
5. Ewert (March 01, 1989).
6. Rothbard (1982).
7. Sherman (May 15, 2019).
8. Bier (September 04, 2015).
9. Goldfine (September 28, 2020).
10. Koenen (September 19, 2013).
11. Crews (May 26, 2020).
12. Sorkin (May 15, 2019).
13. von Mises (1988).
14. Shiller (October 09, 2015); Krugman (December 22, 2018); Stiglitz (May 03, 2019).
15. Higgs (1987).
16. Evans (2004).
17. "Top 30 Innovations of the Last 30 Years." (n.d.) Some of the innovations are part of our everyday experience include, the Internet, PC/laptop computers, mobile phone, email and a couple dozen more.
18. "Top 30 Innovations." (n.d.).
19. "America's Most Innovative Leaders." (2019).
20. "Top 30 Innovations." (n.d.).
21. "Our History." (n.d.).

Chapter 2

1. Tucker (January 16, 2011).
2. Moen and Tallman (n.d.).
3. Google "everything bubble" and an enormous number of links to books, essays, and commentaries highlight the "bubbly" economy and financial markets since the Great Recession.
4. Steelman (October 28, 2020).
5. Jahan, Mahmud, and Papageorgiou (2014; pp. 53–54).

6. Rothbard (1983; p. 282).
7. Rothbard (1983; pp. 252–281).
8. Hazlitt (1959; p. 6).
9. Ebeling (November 1, 2004). See also Rothbard (n.d.). pointed out "*The General Theory* was not truly revolutionary at all but merely old and oft-refuted mercantilist and inflationist fallacies dressed up in shiny new garb, replete with newly constructed and largely incomprehensible jargon."
10. Hazlitt ([1960] 1977).
11. Friedman (1992; p. 49).
12. Friedman (1992; pp. 47–49).
13. According to the Federal Reserve, "Before May 2020, M2 consists of M1 plus (1) savings deposits (including money market deposit accounts); (2) small-denomination time deposits (time deposits in amounts of less than $100,000) less individual retirement account (IRA) and Keogh balances at depository institutions; and (3) balances in retail money market funds (MMFs) less IRA and Keogh balances at MMFs.

    "Beginning May 2020, M2 consists of M1 plus (1) small-denomination time deposits (time deposits in amounts of less than $100,000) less IRA and Keogh balances at depository institutions; and (2) balances in retail MMFs less IRA and Keogh balances at MMFs. Seasonally adjusted M2 is constructed by summing savings deposits (before May 2020), small-denomination time deposits, and retail MMFs, each seasonally adjusted separately, and adding this result to seasonally adjusted M1.

    "For more information on the H.6 release changes and the regulatory amendment that led to the creation of the other liquid deposits component and its inclusion in the M1 monetary aggregate," see the H.6 announcements and Technical Q&As posted on December 17, 2020. Source, https://fred.stlouisfed.org/series/M2#0.

    Also, "M1 includes funds that are readily accessible for spending. M1 consists of: (1) currency outside the U.S. Treasury, Federal Reserve Banks, and the vaults of depository institutions; (2) traveler's checks of nonbank issuers; (3) demand deposits; and (4) other checkable deposits (OCDs), which consist primarily of negotiable order of withdrawal (NOW) accounts at depository institutions and credit union share draft accounts. Seasonally adjusted M1 is calculated by summing currency, traveler's checks, demand deposits, and OCDs, each seasonally adjusted separately." Source: https://fred.stlouisfed.org/series/M1.
14. Jahan and Papageorgiou (2014).
15. Freidman (n.d.; p. 48).
16. Rothbard (1963; p. 31).
17. Rothbard (2020; 191ff).
18. Gwartney (2020).

19. Ibid.
20. Shostak (June 25, 2002).
21. Ettlinger and Linden (August 01, 2012).
22. Rothbard (June 09, 2004).
23. Rothbard (n.d.).
24. Mises ([1912] 1971; pp. 261–275).
25. For a comprehensive bibliography of scores of books and essays in the Austrian tradition, see https://mises.org/search-mises?search=business%20 cycles.
26. Oppers (2002).
27. Oppers (2002; p. 8).
28. Mises (July 30, 2014).
29. McIntyre (March 28, 2009).
30. Earle (October 20, 2020).
31. A Google search of the topic resulted in nearly 700 million hits.
32. Rothbard (n.d.; p. 186ff).
33. Bregu (April 30, 2020).

Chapter 3

1. Shostak (November 10, 2020).
2. Lewis (2011).
3. Fleckenstein and Sheehan (2008); and Stockman (2013).
4. Pring (October 08, 2020). Pring points out, "MA [moving average] crossovers by this highly cyclic indicator are then used as buy signals for the stock market. The chart tells us that all six previous signals were followed by a long-term equity rally. In that respect, the thick arrows point up cycles that experienced a recession, whereas the thin ones reflect four slowdowns in the growth rate of the economy. Slowdowns occur where the economy's growth rate decelerates, but not sufficiently to result in a recession. Note that the two recession-associated signals were followed by the longest and strongest advances."
5. Buffett indicator (March 11, 2021).
6. Shostak (March 27, 2017).

Chapter 4

1. DiLorenzo (2002).
2. Erickson (December 01, 2020).
3. Erickson (n.d.).
4. Ibid.
5. Rothbard (n.d.).

6. Rothbard (n.d.).

7. Ibid. 14ff.

8. Ibid. 22–24.

9. Ibid. 26.

10. Richards and Sablik (December 01, 2020) and (Rothbard 2002).

11. Richards and Sablik (n.d.).

12. Rothbard (n.d.;159 ff).

13. Rothbard, *A History,* 186.

14. Ibid. 188ff.

15. Moen and Tallman (December 01, 2020).

16. Moen and Tallman (n.d.). "The Panic of 1907." An overview of the trust companies' operations reveal they provided substantial liquidity to the stock market and thus encouraged speculation, a hallmark of previous banking panics.

17. Ibid.

18. Ibid.

19. Ibid.

20. Rothbard (n.d.; p. 240).

21. Richardson and Romero (December 04, 2015); and Rothbard (n.d.; 252 ff).

22. Rothbard (2017), especially Chapter 9, "The National Civic Federation: Big Business Organized for Progressivism."

23. Rothbard (n.d.; p. 258).

24. (Jim Powell, *Wilson's War: How Woodrow Wilson's Great Blunder Led to Hitler, Lenin, Stalin and World War II* (New York: Crown Forum, 2005).

25. Grant (2015), Chapter 4, Kindle.

26. Grant, *The Forgotten Depression*, Chapter 4, Kindle.

27. Friedman and Schwartz (1963; pp. 189–239), for their description of the early years of the Federal Reserve, especially the contraction of 1920–1921, 231–239.

28. Rothbard (1983), and "The Forgotten Real Estate Boom of the 1920s," accessed, December 07, 2020, www.library.hbs.edu/hc/crises/forgotten.html.

29. Shostak (June 12, 2020) and Shostak (April 6, 2020). Also Thornton (July 10, 2017) and (Thornton September 13, 2013).

30. Aliber and Kindleberger ([1978] 2015).

31. Aliber and Kindleberger (n.d.; p. 19).

32. Ibid. 19.

33. Ibid. 78.

34. Ibid. 143.

35. Shiller (2015).

36. Shostak (November 19, 2013).

37. Fleckenstein with Sheehan (2008; p. 32).

38. Stockman (December 02, 2020); Insana (December 01, 2020).

Chapter 5

1. I am indebted to Hunter Hastings for these insights. Hastings recounts the experience of entrepreneur B. Luddy in an e-mail to me, March 12, 2021. "When Luddy's tradition metal gauge for his metal bending business (restaurant ventilation systems) increased in cost by 60%, he innovated and sourced a new metal form a new location with a thinner gauge and superior performance, when the 'industry standard' told him it couldn't be done."
2. Cain and Stone (November 23, 2020).
3. Salerno (2011).
4. Corrigan (December 11, 2002).
5. Skousen (December 19, 2020).
6. Read (March 03, 2015).
7. Heng, Yu, and He (July 2005).
8. Rothbard ([1962] 1993).
9. Heng, et al. (n.d.; p. 158).
10. Wanklyn and Hochman (December 15, 2020).
11. Guillot (December 15, 2020).
12. "The Importance of Effectively Managing Raw Materials Inventory." (March 05, 2019).
13. "The Importance of Effectively Managing Raw Materials Inventory." (n.d.).
14. Ibid.
15. Livingston (May 18, 2020).
16. Robert Wenzel writing in his daily economic and financial analysis, *EPJ Daily Alert*, has been making this point in the last half of 2020 in his subscription. Wenzel passed away on May 25, 2021 and his insights about the economy will be greatly missed.
17. LePan (August 02, 2019).
18. Ge, Pan, Zuo-Jun Shen, Wu, Yuan, and Zhang (2019).
19. Irwin (December 17, 2020; R13).
20. Davis (December 17, 2020; R5).
21. Lee (October 15, 2020; B13).

Chapter 6

1. What should be the appropriate public policies that contribute to a robust economy has been debated for decades. Suffice it to say, less government interference in the marketplace beyond protecting property rights and prosecuting fraud would yield the optimal output of goods and services for both consumers and producers. In other words, the costs of complying with dubious government rules and regulations as well as heavy taxation take away scarce resources from the mission of every business.

2. For readers who want to drill further down into the employment data, see the following tables and accompanying charts. This comprehensive database will provide employers with the long-term trends in all sectors of the economy. https://fred.stlouisfed.org/release/tables?rid=50&eid=4881#snid=5361

3. These actions can also apply to a pandemic lockdown, which began in early 2000 as governors and mayors mandated business shutdowns. The pandemic "recession" was the result of deliberate public policies, which contracted economic activity, and not the consequence of the Federal Reserve "tightening" money and credit conditions to ward off an overheated economy.

4. "What is the Difference Between a Furlough, a Layoff, and a Reduction in Force?" December 23, 2020.

5. Zeidner (May 02, 2020).

6. Gelles (November 06, 2020).

7. "Out of Work in America." (October 23, 2020).

8. Uviebinene (December 26, 2019).

9. Williams (December 23, 2020).

10. Uviebinene (n.d.).

11. Ibid.

12. Williams (n.d.).

13. Seth (January 07, 2020).

14. "High Five: The Best Examples of Intrapreneurship in Action." (August 13, 2015). Also see, Smedley (March 12, 2014).

15. "Five Insights Into Intrapreneurship." (January 04, 2021).

16. "Five Insights Into Intrapreneurship." (n.d.).

17. Crippen (September 13, 2013).

18. Patrick (December 23, 2020).

19. Burley (December 23, 2020).

20. Cheng, Dohrmann, Kerlin, and Ramaswamy (July 03, 2018).

21. Feintzeig (October 12, 2020, p. A11).

22. Walden (June 05, 2019).

Chapter 7

1. McMaken (April 08, 2014).

2. "Economics of Value vs. Economies of Scale." (February 01, 2021).

3. Bylund and Hastings (December 03, 2019).

4. Quain (November 08, 2018).

5. Quain (n.d.).

6. Adams (December 19, 2017).

7. Dakin (November 06, 2018).

8. "The Advantages and Disadvantages of the International Expansion." (November 05, 2019).

9. Jackson (February 01, 2021).

10. French (July 17, 2018).

11. Rennert and Schnabl (April 22, 2019).

12. Patel (February 25, 2021).

13. "Our Values." (February 10, 2021).

14. Guynn (April 10, 2012).

15. Stevens and Gasparro (June 16, 2017).

16. Kubota (March 27, 2018).

17. Stoll (November 27, 2020).

18. Stoll (n.d.).

19. Buffett (October 16, 2008).

Chapter 8

1. Carter (January 03, 2021).

2. Hastings and Klein (March 20, 2019).

3. Hastings and Klein (n.d.).

4. Bylund (July 23, 2018).

5. Bylund (n.d.).

6. McMaken (March 13, 2019).

7. "Annual business survey release provides data on minority and women owned businesses." (February 08, 2021).

8. Esposito (May 2019).

9. Sweeney (April 21, 2019).

10. Sweeney (n.d.).

11. Sullivan (July 23, 2003).

12. Ward (April 20, 2020); Duff (February 08, 2021).

13. Crockett (April 11, 2020).

14. The 2020 pandemic has had widespread impacts on small businesses around the country. Several were profiled at the end of 2020. Cowley and Haimrel (December 25, 2020, p. B6–7).

15. I am indebted to Hunter Hastings for pointing this out. Email, March 02, 2021.

16. Obviously selling the business during a business cycle boom would maximize the value to the owner.

17. Lorber (September 11, 2008).

18. Thornton (2018). Also, see https://mises.org/library/housing-bubble-4-easy-steps

19. Thornton, Skyscraper *Curse,* 177ff.

20. D'Angelo (August 10, 2020).
21. King (September 06, 2020, 6L).
22. Simon (August 20, 2020).
23. Simon (n.d.).
24. Charles (April 29, 2018).
25. "13 Types of Insurance of Small Business Owners Should Have." (February 09, 2021).
26. Pacheco (July 31, 2020); and Rockeman, Pickert and Saraiva (October 11, 2020).

Chapter 9

1. Rothbard (1983), 193ff.
2. Rothbard (1983).
3. Kleintop (2021).
4. Cooke, Rose, Otrok, and Owyang (April 16, 2015).
5. Aliber and Kindleberger (2017, p. 200ff).
6. Aliber and Kindleberger (2015).
7. Ibid. 341.
8. Ibid. 357.
9. Ibid. 341.
10. United States Census Bureau (December 2020).
11. United Nations (2021).
12. Bertolo (2016).
13. Bertolo (2016).
14. Ibid.
15. Hannon and Jeong (2021).
16. Hannon and Jeong (2021).
17. Hess (2021).
18. Hess (2021).
19. Bobrow (November 11, 2020).
20. Bobrow (2020).
21. Ibid.
22. Warren Buffett's Letter to Shareholders (February 02, 2021).
23. CNBC (February 02, 2021).
24. Zweig (August 29–30, 2020; p. B4).
25. Export-Import Bank of the United States (February 02, 2021).
26. Office of the United States Trade Representative (February 02, 2021).

Chapter 10

1. Stockman (2013).
2. Smith and Earle (November 20, 2019).
3. Smith and Earle (n.d.).
4. PitchBook (2021).
5. Bylund (July 18, 2018).
6. CNBC (March 11, 2021).
7. CNBC (July 22, 2020).
8. Peterman (June 22, 2020).
9. Bresciani-Turroni (1968) is a classic case study of the German Weimar hyperinflation of the early 1920s.
10. Woods, Jr., (October 11, 2006).
11. Nielsen (Fall 2005).
12. von Mises (1966) and Rothbard (1983) and other works that can be found here.
13. Most economists point out that deflation is "bad" for the economy because it gets out of control as consumers delay spending waiting for lower prices and thus production slows down as demand is reduced.
14. Williams (August 14, 2020).
15. Macovei (October 17, 2019) and Schnabl and Murai (February 25, 2021).
16. Beilfuss (August 17, 2020; p. 30).
17. Farrell (August 25, 2019).

References

Adams, R.L. December 19, 2017. "15 Strategies for Quickly Expanding Your Business. *Entrepreneur*, www.entrepreneur.com/article/306049

Aliber, R.Z., and C.P. Kindleberger. 2015. *Manias, Panics, And Crashes: A History of Financial Crises*, 7th ed. New York, NY: Palgrave Macmillan.

Beilfuss, L. August 17, 2020. "Stagflation Looms Over This Market." *Barron's*.

Ben & Jerry's. 2021. "Our Values." www.benjerry.com/values (accessed February 10, 2021).

Bertolo, T. 2016. "5 Reasons Why U.S. Companies Should Export." *Export-Import Bank of the United States*, https://grow.exim.gov/blog/five-reasons-why-us-companies-should-export

Bier, D. September 04, 2015. "Jimmy Carter Was a Better President than You Think." *FEE*, https://fee.org/articles/jimmy-carter-was-a-better-president-than-you-think/?__cf_chl_jschl_tk__=c32baef34ac32d232b6b70175
dab2a7b0621f94f-1615216373-0-AR5R-gl2gxOF2FZLr5PuFliCr1T
gyGe1ULzsLO4xhg7N10HkAVika9zjicZpbDZ6dSPdixIP1SCG33k
9atClPxDeLlHXuJyGSZU4czWaABhGeR6Vtvd2Df01Jzj87W7CkG
aDPN3y0kZdPI3slZV2ynRA7JMIpcpbEgBohsDP0bN2_35odUeXP
xJNMdLxT-SSPIglpbGpblerybNsnaflkuwe3eXxYEzIgP6nrU-nJWKg-
9PJd4bPquHeLgshmRci2YAF8eAoheeD-ucACDIHd7f8BT57_IiR
SzcnV8WBIrIwvZTpNnApuMvz0NOdHE3P-tJ2HAJ5K99_7ReJ_
AmXixsfr5E4uyKBqrs7Foi0WQe5jZMbaXESeB5du1b9O9cq-
y8zmKZ77iAAwmYQqOQj0mew

Bobrow, E. November 11, 2020. "How Leonard Lauder Built Estée Lauder Into a Cosmetics Behemoth." *The Wall Street Journal*, www.wsj.com/articles/how-leonard-lauder-built-estee-lauder-into-a-cosmetics-behemoth-11605891079?mod=searchresults_pos12&page=2

Bregu, K. April 30, 2020. "The Fed is Running Out of Bubbles to Create." *Mises Wire*, https://mises.org/wire/fed-running-out-bubbles-create

Bresciani-Turroni, C. [1937] 1968 . *The Economics of Inflation: A Study of Currency Depreciation in Post-War Germany*, Trans. M.E. Savers. Northampton: Augustus M. Kelley.

Buffett, W. October 16, 2008. "Buy American. I am." *New York Times*, www.nytimes.com/2008/10/17/opinion/17buffett.html

Burley, K. 2020. "How to Maintain an Effective Workforce." *Chron*, https://smallbusiness.chron.com/maintain-effective workforce20662.html (accessed December 23, 2020).

Bylund, P. July 18, 2018. "You May Run From It, But Disruption Is Going To Occur All The Same—Here's How To Embrace Change." *Entrepreneur*, www.entrepreneur.com/article/316910

Bylund, P. July 23, 2018. "Most Entrepreneurs Are Bad Entrepreneurs." *Mises Wire*, https://mises.org/wire/most-entrepreneurs-are-bad-entrepreneurs.

Bylund, P., and H. Hastings. December 03, 2019. "Per Bylund on the 'Economics of Value versus Economies of Scale.'" *Economics for Business*, https://mises. org/library/bylund-economics-value-versus-economies-scale

Cain, A., and M. Stone. November 23, 2020. "These 38 Retailers and Restaurant Companies have Filed for Bankruptcy or Liquidation in 2020." *Business Insider*, www.businessinsider.com/retailers-filed-bankruptcy-liquidation-closing-stores-2020-2

Capital. 2021. "The Advantages and Disadvantages of the International Expansion." (accessed February 01, 2021). www.capital-ges.com/the-advantages-and-disadvantages-of-international-expansion/

Carter, T. January 03, 2021. "The True Failure Rate of Small Businesses." *Entrepreneur*, www.entrepreneur.com/article/361350

Charles, J. April 29, 2018. "9 Things You Must Do Today to Grow Your Small Business." *Small Business Trends*, www.smallbiztrends.com/2018/04/how-to-grow-your-small-business.html

Cheng, W.L., T. Dohrmann, M. Kerlin, and S. Ramaswamy. July 03, 2018. "Creating An Effective Workforce System for the New Economy." *McKinsey & Company*, www.mckinsey.com/industries/public-and-social-sector/our-insights/creating-an-effective-workforce-system-for-the-new-economy

CMI. August 13, 2015. "High Five: The Best Examples of Intrapreneurship in Action." www.managers.org.uk/knowledge-and-insights/article/high-five-the-best-examples-of-intrapreneurship-in-action/

CNBC. March 11, 2021. "A Look Back at the CNBC Disruptor 50: 8 Years, 209 Companies." www.cnbc.com/2020/06/16/a-look-back-at-the-cnbc-disruptor-50-8-years-209-companies.html

CNBC. 2021. "Berkshire Hathaway Portfolio Tracker." www.cnbc.com/berkshire-hathaway-portfolio/ (accessed February 02, 2021).

CNBC. July 22, 2020. "These Are the 2020 CNBC Disruptor 50 Companies." www.cnbc.com/2020/06/16/meet-the-2020-cnbc-disruptor-50-companies.html

Cooke, D.A., and M.A. Rose, C. Otrok, and M.T. Owyang. April 16, 2015. "How Are Countries Business Cycles Moving Together These Days." *Regional Economist*, www.stlouisfed.org/publications/regional-economist/april-2015/regional-versus-global-business-cycles

Corrigan, S. December 11, 2002. "The Cone of Production." *Mises Daily Articles*, https://mises.org/library/cone-production

Cowley, S., and A. Haimrel. December 25, 2020. "Thriving In a Pandemic, But Feeling Survivors Guilt." *New York Times.*

Crews, C.W. May 26, 2020. "Ten Thousand Commandments 2020." *Competitive Enterprise Institute,* https://cei.org/studies/ten-thousand-commandments-2020/

Crippen, A. September 13, 2013. "Warren Buffett Shares His Secret: How You Can 'Tap Dance to Work.'" *CNBC,* www.cnbc.com/2012/11/21/warren-buffett-shares-his-secret-how-you-can-tap-dance-to-work.html

Crockett, Z. April 11, 2020. "How Small Business Owners Survived the Great Recession." *The Hustle,* https://thehustle.co/small-business-owners-great-recession-covid19/

Current Market Valuation. March 11, 2021. "Buffett Indicator: Strongly Overvalued." www.currentmarketvaluation.com/models/buffett-indicator.php

D'Angelo, M. August 10, 2020. "Tips on Choosing the Right Location for your Business." *Business News Daily,* www.businessnewsdaily.com/15760-choosing-business-location.html

Dakin, J. November 06, 2018. "Growing And Expanding Your Business." *Forbes,* www.forbes.com/sites/jordandaykin/2018/11/06/growing-and-expanding-your-business/?sh=50f87511d6a6

Davis, S. December 17, 2020. "Made in America." *The Wall Street Journal.*

DeFranco, K.J., Jr. May 20, 2015. "The Coca-Cola Company: A Short SWOT Analysis. *Value Line.* www.valueline.com/Stocks/Highlights/The_Coca-Cola_CompanyA_Short_SWOT_Analysis.aspx#.YEY3kC2ZOHs

Deloitte Digital. 2021. "Five Insights Into Intrapreneurship: A Guide to Accelerating Innovation Within Corporations." www2.deloitte.com/content/dam/Deloitte/de/Documents/technology/Intrapreneurship_Whitepaper_English.pdf (accessed January 04, 2021).

DemandCaster. March 05, 2019. "The Importance of Effectively Managing Raw Materials Inventory." www.demandcaster.com/blog/the-importance-of-effectively-managing-raw-materials-inventory/

DiLorenzo, T.J. 2002. *The Real Lincoln: A New Look at Abraham Lincoln, His Agenda, and an Unnecessary War.* Roseville, CA: Prima Publishing.

Duff, V. 2021. "How to Offset The Downswing In The Business Cycle." *Chron.* https://smallbusiness.chron.com/offset-downswing-business-cycle-10419.html (accessed February 08, 2021).

Earle, P.C. 2020. "US Presidents and the Federal Reserve." *Museum of American Finance.* www.moaf.org/publications-collections/financial-history-magazine/131/_res/id=Attachments/index=0/US%20Presidents%20and%20the%20Federal%20Reserve.pdf (accessed October 20, 2020).

Ebeling, R.M. November 01, 2004. "Henry Hazlitt and the Failure of Keynesian Economics." *FEE,* https://fee.org/articles/henry-hazlitt-and-the-failure-of-keynesian-economics/

Esposito, N. May 2019. "Small Business Facts: Spotlight on Minority Owned Employer Businesses." *U.S. Small Business Administration*, https://cdn. advocacy.sba.gov/wp-content/uploads/2019/05/31131339/Small-Business-Facts-Spotlight-on-Minority-Owned-Employer-Businesses.pdf.

Ewert, K.S. March 01, 1989. "Moral Criticisms of the Market." *The Freeman*, https://fee.org/articles/moral-criticisms-of-the-market/

Ettlinger, M., and M. Linden. August 01, 2012. "The Failure of Supply Side Economics." *Center for American Progress*, https://www.americanprogress. org/issues/economy/news/2012/08/01/11998/the-failure-of-supply-side-economics/

Evans, H., with G. Buckland, and D. Lefer. 2004. *They Made America*. New York: Little, Brown and Company.

Export-Import Bank of the United States. 2021. "10 Free Tools to Help You Become an Expert in Exporting." https://grow.exim.gov/export-expertise? hsCtaTracking=845c5553-b8d3-41ae-a8df-fd607d6dd090%7C598c5413-dc80-4d13-bd23-19bb763833ac (accessed February 02, 2021).

Farrell, C. August 25, 2019. "Is an Aging Population Hurting the U.S. Economy?" *Forbes*, www.forbes.com/sites/nextavenue/2019/08/25/is-an-aging-population-hurting-the-u-s-economy/?sh=6256d7f33aa1

Feintzeig, R. October 12, 2020. "How Managers Can Rally the Troops." *The Wall Street Journal*.

Fleckenstein, W.A., and F. Sheehan. 2008. *Greenspan's Bubbles: The Age of Ignorance at the Federal Reserve*. New York, NY: McGraw-Hill Education.

Forbes. September 2019. "America's Most Innovative Leaders." www.forbes.com/ lists/innovative-leaders/#fef5b6126aa9

Forbes. 2021. "13 Types of Insurance of Small Business Owners Should Have." www.forbes.com/sites/thesba/2012/01/19/13-types-of-insurance-a-small-business-owner-should-have/?sh=9dc6a9e20d39 (accessed February 09, 2021).

Forbes. February 19, 2009. "Top 30 Innovations of the Last 30 Years." www. forbes.com/2009/02/19/innovation-internet-health-entrepreneurs-technology_wharton.html?sh=7a6c3a8b2b2f

French, D. July 17, 2018. "Big Corporate Mergers Often Come with Big Risks." *Mises Institute*, https://mises.org/power-market/big-corporate-mergers-often-come-big-risks

Friedman, M. 1992. *Money Mischief: Episodes in Monetary History*. New York, NY: Harcourt Brace Jovanovich.

Ge, D., Y. Pan, Y., Z.J.M. Shen, D. Wu, R. Yuan, and C. Zhang. 2019. "Retail Supply Chain Management: A Review of Theories and Practices." *Journal of Data, Information and Management* 1, 45–64. https://doi.org/10.1007/s42488-019-00004-z

Gelles, D. November 06, 2020. "The C.E.O. Who Promised there Would be No Layoffs." *New York Times,* www.nytimes.com/2020/11/06/business/corner-office-ajay-banga-mastercard.html

Goldfine, L. September 28, 2020. "Here's Every Company that went Bankrupt During COVID-19." *B2-The Business of Business,* https://media.thinknum.com/articles/coronavirus-bankruptcies-chapter-11-filing-hertz-neiman-marcus-jc-penney-data/

Grant, J. 2015. *The Forgotten Depression: 1921: The Crash That Cured Itself.* New York, NY: Simon & Schuster, Kindle.

Guillot, C. November 18, 2019. "Managing Supply Chain Risk in an Economic Downturn." *Supply Chain Dive,* www.supplychaindive.com/news/managing-supply-chain-risk-in-an-economic- downturn/567535/

Gwartney, J.D. 2020. "Supply Side Economics." *Econolib,* www.econlib.org/library/Enc/SupplySideEconomics.html (accessed October 20, 2020).

Guynn, J. April 10, 2012. "Insta-Rich: $1 Billion for Instagram." *Los Angeles Times,* www.latimes.com/business/la-xpm-2012-apr-10-la-fi-tn-how-kevin-systrom-built-instagram20120410-story.html

Hannon, P., and E.Y. Jeong. January 24, 2021. "China Overtakes U.S. as World's Leading Destination for Foreign Direct Investment." The *Wall Street Journal,* www.wsj.com/articles/china-overtakes-u-s-as-worlds-leading-destination-for-foreign-direct-investment-11611511200

Hastings, H., and P.G. Klein. March 20, 2019. "Peter Klein on Entrepreneurial Empathy." *Economics of Business,* https://mises.org/library/peter-klein-entrepreneurial-empathy

Harvard Business School, Historical Collections. 2020. "The Forgotten Real Estate Boom of the 1920s." www.library.hbs.edu/hc/crises/forgotten.html (accessed December 07, 2020).

Hazlitt, H., ed. [1960] 1977. *The Critics of Keynesian Economics.* New Rochelle: Arlington House.

Hazlitt, H. 1959. *The Failure of the "New Economics": An Analysis of the Keynesian Fallacies.* New Rochelle, NY: Arlington House.

Hayek, F.A. [1934] 1967. *Prices and Production.* New York, NY: Augustus M. Kelley.

Heng, M., W. Yu, and X. He. July 2005. "Supply Chain Management and Business Cycles." *Supply Chain Management: An International Journal,* 157–161. https://doi.org/10.1108/13598540510578324

Hess, R. 2021. "Ten Business Strategies For Multinationals Amid US– China Trade Tensions." *Newmark,* www.ngkfgcs.com/Blog/September-2019/10-Business-Strategies-For-Multinationals-US-China (accessed February 02, 2021).

Higgs, R. 1987. *Crisis and Leviathan: Critical Episodes in the Growth of American Government.* New York, NY: Oxford University Press.

Insana, R. July 09, 2020. "Main Street Investors Diving into Speculative Penny Stocks and SPACs is Disturbing Trend." www.cnbc.com/2020/07/09/op-ed-main-street-investors-diving-into-speculative-penny-stocks-and-spacs-is-disturbing-trend.html

Irwin, D.A. December 17, 2020. "Globalization in Retreat." *The Wall Street Journal.*

Jackson, J. 2021. "Why do up to 90% of Mergers and Acquisitions Fail." *Business Chief,* www.businesschief.eu/corporate-finance/wdo-90-mergers-and-acquisitions-fail

Jahan, S., A.S. Mahmud, and C. Papageorgiou. 2014. "What Is Keynesian Economics?" *Finance & Development* 51, no. 3, 53–54. www.imf.org/external/pubs/ft/fandd/2014/09/basics.htm

Jurevicius, O. February 13, 2013. "SWOT Analysis-Do it Properly!" *Strategic Management Insight,* https://strategicmanagementinsight.com/tools/swot-analysis-how-to-do-it.html

Kearney. 2020. "High Inflation: Unchartered Waters for Supply Management." www.nl.kearney.com/procurement/article/?/a/high-inflation-uncharted-waters-for-supply-management (accessed December 15, 2020).

King, R. September 06, 2020. "Drive to Survive." *The Record.*

Kleintop, J. November 23, 2020. "2021 Global Outlook: New Cycle, New Leadership." *Charles Schwab Advisor Services,* https://advisorservices.schwab.com/content/2021-global-outlook-new-cycle-new-leadership

Koenen, K.J. September 19, 2013. "Warren Buffett: 'America works,' But Income Gap Fears are Real (Video)." *Washington Business Journal,* www.bizjournals.com/washington/blog/2013/09/warren-buffett-extols-resiliency-of.html

Krugman, P. December 22, 2018. "The Case for a Mixed Economy." *New York Times,* www.nytimes.com/2018/12/22/opinion/the-case-for-a-mixed-economy.html

Kubota, Y. March 27, 2018. "Unit of Taiwan's Foxconn to buy Los Angeles–Based Belkin." *The Wall Street Journal,* www.wsj.com/articles/unit-of-taiwans-foxconn-to-buy-los-angeles-based-belkin-1522151550

Lee, J. October 15, 2020. "Cool Places for Clothes Sell Groceries." *The Wall Street Journal.*

LePan, N. August 02, 2019. "What is a Commodity Super Cycle?" www.visualcapitalist.com/what-is-a-commodity-super-cycle/

Lewis, M. 2010. *The Big Short: Inside the Doomsday Machine.* New York, NY: W.W. Norton.

Livingston, A. May 18, 2020. "'All of the Party Was Over': How the Last Oil Bust Changed Texas." *Texas Tribune,* www.texastribune.org/2020/05/18/texas-oil-prices-1980s/

Lorber, L. September 11, 2008. "Ways to Cash Out of Your Business." *The Wall Street Journal*, www.wsj.com/articles/BL-HOWTOSBB-9

Macovei, M. October 17, 2019. "Stimulus Brings Stagnation: The Case of Japan." *Mises Wire*, https://mises.org/wire/stimulus-brings-stagnation-case-japan.

McDonald's. 2020."Our History." www.mcdonalds.com/us/en-us/about-us/our-history.html (accessed October 10, 2020).

McIntyre, D.A. 2020. "The 10 American Companies With the Most Cash." *24/7 Wall St.*, https://247wallst.com/investing/2020/03/28/the-10-american-companies-with-the-most-cash/

McMaken, R. April 08, 2014. "Extended Version of Peter Klein's Interview on Entrepreneurship." *Mises Wire*, https://mises.org/wire/extended-version-peter-kleins-interview-entrepreneurship

McMaken, R. March 13, 2019. "Small Businesses Are Key in Improving the Lives of Workers." *Mises Wire,* https://mises.org/wire/small-businesses-are-key-improving-lives-workers

MindTools.com. 2021. "SWOT Analysis: How to Develop a Strategy for Success." www.mindtools.com/pages/article/newTMC_05.htm (accessed March 02, 2021).

Mises Institute. 2021. "Economics of Value vs. Economies of Scale." https://cdn.mises.org/Economics%20of%20Value%20vs.%20Economies%20of%20Scale.pdf (accessed February 01, 2021).

Moen, J.R., and E.W. Tallman. December 04, 2015. "The Panic of 1907." *Federal Reserve History,* www.federalreservehistory.org/essays/panic_of_1907

Moss, B.H. June 01, 2012. "How to Build a Workforce, One Person at a Time," *SHRM®*, www.shrm.org/hr-today/news/hr-magazine/pages/0612moss.aspx

Nielsen, E. Fall 2005. "Monetary Policy In The Confederacy." *Region Focus*, www.richmondfed.org//media/richmondfedorg/publications/research/econ_focus/2005/fall/pdf/economic_history.pdf

Oppers, S.E. January 01, 2002. "The Austrian Theory of Business Cycles: Old Lesson for Modern Economic Policy?" *IMF Working Papers*, www.imf.org/en/Publications/WP/Issues/2016/12/30/The-Austrian-Theory-of-Business-Cycles-Old-Lessons-for-Modern-Economic-Policy-15480

Office of the United States Trade Representative. 2021. "Free Trade Agreements." https://ustr.gov/trade-agreements/free-trade-agreements (accessed February 02, 2021).

Pacheco, I. July 31, 2020. "Immigrant-Owned Business Are Especially Hard-Hit Amid The Pandemic." *The Wall Street Journal*, www.wsj.com/articles/immigrant-owned-businesses-are-especially-hard-hit-amid-the-pandemic-11596187802?mod=searchresults_pos17&page=1

Patel, K. February 25, 2021. "The 8 Biggest M&A Failures of All Time." *Deal Room*, https://dealroom.net/blog/biggest-mergers-and-acquisitions-failures

Patrick, M. 2020. "Secrets to Motivating Your Team." *Chron*, https://smallbusiness.chron.com/secrets-motivating-team-30743.html (accessed December 23, 2020).

Peterman, S. June 22, 2020. "Central Bankers Will Bring Us Economic Stagnation." *Mises Wire*, https://mises.org/wire/central-bankers-will-bring-us-economic-stagnation

PitchBook. 2021. "US Private Equity Activity Rebounded To Healthy Levels In 2020 Despite Covid–19 Headwinds." https://pitchbook.com/media/press-releases/us-private-equity-activity-rebounded-to-healthy-levels-in-2020-despite-covid-19-headwinds (accessed February 19, 2021).

Powell, J. 2005. *Wilson's War: How Woodrow Wilson's Great Blunder Led to Hitler, Lenin, Stalin and World War II*. New York, NY: Crown Forum.

Pring, M. October 08, 2020. "Reliable Long – Term Ratio May Be About to Trigger Its Seventh Buy Signal for Stocks Since 1995." *Stockcharts.com*, https://stockcharts.com/articles/chartwatchers/2020/10/reliable-longterm-ratio-may-be-630.html

Quain, S. November 08, 2018. "The Advantages of Expanding Business." *Chron*, https://smallbusiness.chron.com/advantages-expanding-business-21144.html

Read, L. March 03, 2015. "I, Pencil." *Foundation for Economic Education*, https://fee.org/articles/i-pencil/

Rennert, P., and G. Schnabl. April 22, 2019. "Central Banks May Be Enabling Unhealthy Corporate Buyouts." *Mises Wire*, https://mises.org/power-market/big-corporate-mergers-often-come-big-risks

Richards, G., and T. Sablik. 2020. "Banking Panics of the Gilded Age." *Federal Reserve History*, www.federalreservehistory.org/essays/banking-panics-of-the-gilded-age (accessed December 01, 2020).

Richardson, G., and J. Romero. December 04, 2015. "The Meeting at Jekyll Island: November 20, 1910-November 30, 1910." *Federal Reserve History*, federalreservehistory.org/essays/jekyll-island-conference

Rockeman, O., R. Pickert, and C. Saraiva. October 11, 2020. "Falling Behind." *The Record*.

Rothbard, M.N. 2002. *A History of Money and Banking in the United States: The Colonial Era to World War II*. Auburn, AL: Ludwig von Mises Institute.

Rothbard, M.N. [1963] 1983. *America's Great Depression*. New York: Richardson & Snyder.

Rothbard, M.N. [1963] 2009. *Economic Depressions: Their Cause and Cure*. Auburn, AL: Ludwig von Mises Institute, https://cdn.mises.org/Economic%20Depressions%20Their%20Cause%20and%20Cure_4.pdf

Rothbard, M.N. 2010. *Keynes the Man*. Auburn, AL: Ludwig von Mises Institute, https://cdn.mises.org/Keynes%20the%20Man_2.pdf.

Rothbard, M.N. 1982. "Law, Property Rights, and Air Pollution. *Cato Journal* 2, no. 1, pp. 55–99.

Rothbard, M.N. [1962] 1993. *Man. Economy and State: A Treatise on Economic Principles*. Auburn, AL: Ludwig von Mises Institute.

Rothbard, M.N. 1970. *Power and Market: Government and the Economy*. Menlo Park, CA: Institute for Humane Studies.

Rothbard, M.N. June 06, 2004. "The Myth of Reaganomics." *Mises Daily Articles*, https://mises.org/library/myths-reaganomics

Rothbard, M.N. 2020. "The Panic of 1819." https://mises.org/library/panic-1819-reactions-and-policies (accessed October 20, 2020).

Rothbard, M.N. 2017. *The Progressive Era*. Auburn, AL: Mises Institute.

Rothbard, M.N. 1963. *What Has Government Done to Our Money?* Auburn, AL: Ludwig von Mises Institute.

Salerno, J.T. 2011. "A Reformulation of Austrian Business Cycle Theory in Light of the Financial Crisis." *The Quarterly Journal of Austrian Economics* 15, no. 1, 8–9. https://cdn.mises.org/qjae15_1_1.pd

Sarwat, J., and C. Papageorgiou. 2014. "What is Monetarism." *Finance & Development*, 51 no. 1. www.imf.org/external/pubs/ft/fandd/2014/03/basics.htm

Schnabl, G., and T. Murai. February 25, 2021. "Japan's Well-Fed Zombie Corporations." *Mises Wire*, https://mises.org/wire/japans-well-fed-zombie-corporations

Seth, A. January 07, 2020. "Intro to Intrapreneurship: An Alternate Path to Entrepreneurship with Steady Income." www.andyseth.com/2020/01/07/intro-intrapreneurship-alternate-path-entrepreneurship-steady-income/

Sherman, T. May 15, 2019. "The 50 School Districts that Spend the Most Per Student in N.J." *NJ.com*, www.nj.com/education/2017/05/the_50_school_districts_that_spend_the_most_per_pu.html

Shiller, R.J. October 09, 2015. "Faith in Unregulated Free Market? Don't Fall for It." *New York Times*, www.nytimes.com/2015/10/11/upshot/faith-in-an-unregulated-free-market-dont-fall-for-it.html

Shiller, R.J. 2015. *Irrational Exuberance*, 3rd ed. Princeton: Princeton University Press, Kindle.

Shostak, F. November 19, 2013. "Are Bubbles Caused by Psychological Problems?" *Mises Daily Articles*, https://mises.org/library/are-bubbles-caused-psychological-problems

Shostak, F. April 06, 2020. "Creating More Money Won't Revive the Economy." *Mises Wire*, https://mises.org/wire/creating-more-money-wont-revive-economy

Shostak, F. November 10, 2020. "How Easy Money Creates the Boom-Bust Cycle." *Mises Wire*, https://mises.org/wire/how-easy-money-creates-boom-bust-cycle

Shostak, F. March 27, 2017. "How to Interpret the Shape of the Yield Curve." *Mises Wire*, https://mises.org/wire/how-interpret-shape-yield-curve

Shostak, F. June 12, 2020. "Savings Are Critical to a Prosperous Economy." *Mises Wire*, https://mises.org/wire/savings-are-critical-prosperous-economy

Shostak, F. June 25, 2002. "The Supply-Side Gold Standard: A Critique." *Mises Daily Articles.* https://mises.org/library/supply-side-gold-standard-critique

SHRM®. 2020. "What is the Difference Between a Furlough, a Layoff, and a Reduction in Force?" www.shrm.org/resourcesandtools/tools-and-samples/hr-qa/pages/furloughlayoffreductioninforce.aspx (accessed December 23, 2020).

Simon, R. August 20, 2020. "Covid-19 Shuttered More Than 1 Small Businesses. Here Is How Five Survived." *The Wall Street Journal*, www.wsj.com/articles/covid-19-shuttered-more-than-1-million-small-businesses-here-is-how-five-survived-11596254424?mod=searchresults_pos6&page=1

Skousen, M. 2020. "Gross Output." https://grossoutput.com/gross-output/ (accessed December 19, 2020).

Smedley, T. March 12, 2014. "'Intrapreneurs' come to the rescue." *Financial Times*, www.ft.com/content/556c3a46-8fdf-11e3-aee9-00144feab7de

Smith, S.S., and P.C. Earle. November 20, 2019. "The Demonization of Private Equity." *American Institute for Economic Research*, www.aier.org/article/the-demonization-of-private-equity/

Sorkin, A.R. May 15, 2019. "Warren Buffett's Case for Capitalism." *New York Times*, www.nytimes.com/2019/05/05/business/warren-buffett-capitalism.html

Special Section. October 23, 2020. "Out of Work in America." *New York Times.*

Steelman, A. 2020. "Full Employment and Balance Budget Act of 1978 (Humphrey-Hawkins)." *Federal Reserve History,* www.federalreservehistory.org/essays/humphrey-hawkins-act (accessed October 28, 2020).

Stevens, L., and A. Gasparro. June 16, 2017. "Amazon to Buy Whole Foods for $13.7 Billion." *The Wall Street Journal*, www.wsj.com/articles/amazon-to-buy-whole-foods-for-13-7-billion-1497618446

Stiglitz, J.E. May 03, 2019. "The Economy We Need." *Project Syndicate*, www.project-syndicate.org/onpoint/the-economy-we-need-by-joseph-e-stiglitz-2019-05?barrier=accesspaylog

Stockman, D.A. 2021. "David Stockman on The Coming Financial Panic and the 2020 Election." Interview by Doug Casey, *International Man*, https://internationalman.com/articles/david-stockman-on-the-coming-financial-panic-and-the-2020-election/ (accessed, February 15, 2021).

Stockman, D.A. 2013. *The Great Deformation: The Corruption of Capitalism In America.* New York: Public Affairs.

Stoll, J.D. November 27, 2020. "Mirror Entrepreneur Sold Her Fitness Startup to Lululemon. Letting Go, Meant Sticking Around." *The Wall Street Journal,* www.wsj.com/articles/mirror-entrepreneur-sold-her-fitness-startup-to-lululemon-letting-go-meant-sticking-around-11606492843

Sullivan, T. July 23, 2003. "Business Cycle Affects Small Firms." *Insperity,* https://m.smallbusinessadvocate.com/small-business-article/business-cycle-affects small-firms-dot-dot-dot-597

Sweeney, D. April 21, 2019. "4 Cash Flow Challenges Facing Small-Business Owners Today." *Forbes,* www.forbes.com/sites/allbusiness/2019/04/21/cash-flow-challenges-facing-small-business-owners/?sh=55e0371b3656

Thornton, M. September 13, 2013. "Only Austrian Theory Can Explain and Expose Booms and Bubbles." *Mises Daily Articles,* https://mises.org/library/only-austrian-theory-can-explain-and-expose-booms-and-bubbles

Thornton, M. July 10, 2017. "The Bernanke-Yellen Bubble-Depression." *Mises Wire,* https://mises.org/wire/bernanke-yellen-bubble-depression.

Thornton, M. 2018. *The Skyscraper Curse: And How Austrian Economist Predicted Every Major Economic Crisis of the Last Century.* Auburn, AL: Mises Institute.

Tucker, J.A. January 16, 2011. "Operation Panic: Mises Wiki." *Mises Wire,* https://mises.org/wire/operation-panic-mises-wiki

United Nations. 2021. "Key Statistics and Trends in International Trade 2020." https://unctad.org/system/files/official-document/ditctab2020d4_en.pdf (accessed February 23, 2021).

United States Census Bureau. 2021. "Annual Business Survey Release Provides Data on Minority and Women Owned Businesses." www.census.gov/newsroom/press-releases/2020/annual-business-survey-data.html (accessed February 08, 2021).

United States Census Bureau. December 2020. "Monthly U.S. International Trade in Goods and Services." www.census.gov/foreign-trade/Press-Release/2020pr/ft900_2012.pdf (accessed February 08, 2021).

Uviebinene, E. December 26, 2019. "'Intrapreneurs' Are the People Driving Corporate Change." *The Financial Times,* www.ft.com/content/fb6c6008-2181-11ea-b8a1-584213ee7b2b

von Mises, L. July 30, 2014. "Comments About the Mathematical Treatment of Economic Problems." *Mises Institute,* https://mises.org/library/comments-about-mathematical-treatment-economic-problems-1

von Mises, L. 1966. *Human Action: A Treatise in Economics,* 3rd revised. ed. Chicago: Henry Regnery Company.

von Mises, L. [1940] 1988. *Interventionism: An Economic Analysis.* Irvington-on-Hudson, NY: The Foundation for Economic Education.

Walden, S. June 05, 2019. "Building a Roadmap for Effective Reskilling in the AI-Infused Workplace for Tomorrow." *Dell Technologies,* www.delltechnologies.com/en-us/perspectives/building-a-roadmap-for-effective-reskilling-in-the-ai-infused-workplace-of-tomorrow/

Wanklyn, J., and M. Hochman. 2020. "High Inflation: Unchartered Waters for Supply Management." *Kearney*, www.nl.kearney.com/procurement/article/?/a/high-inflation-uncharted-waters-for-supply-management (accessed December 15, 2020).

Ward, S. April 20, 2020. "7 Ways To Recession-Proof Your Business." *The Balance Small Business*, www.thebalancesmb.com/business-thrive-tough-economy-2948298

Warren Buffett's Letter to Shareholders. 2021. "Berkshire-Past, Present and Future." www.berkshirehathaway.com/SpecialLetters/WEB%20past%20present%20future%202014.pdf (accessed February 02, 2021).

Welch, M., and A. Garcia. December 12, 2018. "When Democrats Loved Deregulation." *Reason*, https://reason.com/2018/12/12/when-democrats-loved-deregulation/

Williams, R. August 14, 2020. "Why Stagflation is Back on Some Traders' Minds." *Bloomberg*, www.bloomberg.com/news/articles/2020-08-14/why-stagflation-is-back-on-some-traders-radars-quicktake

Williams, T. 2020. "Intrapreneurship: Driving Innovation From Within." *The Economist*, https://execed.economist.com/blog/industry-trends/intrapreneurship-driving-innovation-within (accessed December 23, 2020).

Woods, T.E. Jr. October 11, 2006. "The Revolutionary War and the Destruction of the Continental." *Mises Daily Articles*, https://mises.org/library/revolutionary-war-and-destruction-continental

Zeidner, R. 2020. "Cutting Staff in Times of Crisis: Managing Your Team In A Downsized Organization." www.shrm.org/hr-today/news/all-things-work/pages/cutting-staff-due-to-coronavirus-fallout.aspx (accessed December 23, 2020).

Zweig, J. August 29–30, 2020. "Warren Buffett and the $300,000 Haircut." *The Wall Street Journal*.

About the Author

Dr. Murray Sabrin joined the faculty of the Anisfield school of Business of Ramapo College of New Jersey in 1985 and retired on July 01, 2020, as Professor of Finance. Over his career he taught several courses including Corporate Finance, Securities and Investments, and Financial History of the United States. On January 25, 2021, the board of trustees awarded Dr. Sabrin Emeritus status for his scholarship and professional contributions during his 35-year career.

In 2007, the Sabrins made a $250,000 gift to Ramapo College to establish the Sabrin Center for Free Enterprise in the Anisfield School of Business (www.ramapo.edu/sabrincenter), and they made a $50,000 donation to establish the Sabrin Center study room in the Peter F. Mercer Learning Commons that is scheduled to open in the fall 2021.

Dr. Sabrin is considered a "public intellectual" for writing essays about the economy for *The Record, Star-Ledger, Trenton Times*, and the *Asbury Park Press*. He has been a frequent guest on New York, New Jersey, and Connecticut talk radio shows and on national podcasts. His essays have also appeared in *Commerce Magazine, Mid-Atlantic Journal of Business, Nonprofit Management & Leadership,* and *Privatization Review* among other scholarly and popular publications.

Recently, Dr. Sabrin's book, *Universal Medical Care: From Conception to End-of-Life: The Case for a Single Payer System,* was published, outlining his vision for a single payer approach where the individual or family is in charge of their medical decisions. The "individual" single-payer system is based on restoring the doctor-patient relationship as well as other reforms. Sabrin is the author of *Tax Free 2000: The Rebirth of American Liberty,* a blueprint to create a tax-free America in the 21st century, and *Why the Federal Reserve Sucks: It Causes Inflation, Recessions, Bubbles and Enriches the One Percent,* which is available on Amazon.

In 2003, Dr. Sabrin was invited to serve as a founding trustee of the Bergen Volunteer Medical Initiative (BVMI) located in Hackensack, New Jersey, where he served until 2008.

Murray Sabrin arrived in America from West Germany at the age of two with his parents and older brother on August 06, 1949, and became a U.S. citizen in June 1959. His parents were the only members of their respective families to survive the Holocaust. The Sabrin family moved from the Lower East Side of Manhattan to the Bronx in 1953, where they lived until 1977; then he and his wife Florence moved to New Jersey, where they have lived until they moved to Florida in June 2021.

Dr. Sabrin was graduated from the Bronx High School of Science in 1964. He has a BA in history, geography, and social studies education from Hunter College; an MA in social studies education from Lehman College; and a PhD in economic geography from Rutgers University. Sabrin is only one of two individuals who had the honor of having the late Austrian school economist, historian, and philosopher Murray N. Rothbard serve as a member of his dissertation committee. His dissertation, "The Spatial Incidence of Inflation in the United States 1967–1971: An Economic-Geographic Perspective," was reviewed by a University of Chicago professor who stated, "You are to be congratulated on the theoretical and critical depth of your thesis."

In 1997, he was the New Jersey Libertarian Party's nominee for governor and made political history when he raised sufficient funds to participate in the state's matching fund program, which required him to participate in three debates with the two major party candidates. He also has sought the Republican nomination for the U.S. Senate.

Index

CPSIA information can be obtained
at www.ICGtesting.com
Printed in the USA
BVHW041040120222
628730BV00002B/8